INNOVATIVE WEAVING

A Guide for Study Groups

Mickey Stam

Published by

Weavers and Spinners Society of Austin
PO Box 301167
Austin, TX 78703
www.wssaustin.org

Copyright © Mickey Stam

All rights reserved. No part of this book may be reproduced, stored in a retrieval system, or transmitted in any form or by any means, mechanical, photocopying, recording or otherwise, without the prior permission of the copyright owner.

ISBN 13 978 0692657331

Third edition February 2018 (minor updates)
Second edition November 2016 (minor updates)
First edition July 2016

Cover Design: Kelly Guerrero
Front Cover
    Painting: Lynn Putney
    Weaving: Sandra Doak
Back Cover
    Left: Bob Bateman
    Center: Inga Marie Carmel
    Right: Mickey Stam

All photography by Mickey Stam, except where noted.

TABLE OF CONTENTS

FORWARD 5
INTRODUCTION 7
MEETING ONE: GETTING STARTED WITH YOUR STUDY GROUP 9
MEETING TWO: PICTURE IT ON YOUR LOOM 21
MEETING THREE: TRIAL AND ERROR IN THREE DIMENSIONS 29
MEETING FOUR: ALIVE WITH THE SOUND OF MUSIC 41
MEETING FIVE: BUILDING ART INTO YOUR CRAFT 55
MEETING SIX: LET'S PUT ON A SHOW! 69
MEETING SEVEN: WEAVE YOUR PASSION 77
MEETING EIGHT: FOCUS YOUR WEAVING 89
MEETING NINE: FASHION YOURSELF A COLLECTION 101
MEETING TEN: WEAVING FOR THE PUBLIC 113
MEETING ELEVEN: PICTURE IT IN MOTION 125
MEETING TWELVE: INSTALLATION ART AND LEGACY 137
AFTERWORD 149
ACKNOWLEDGEMENTS 151
INDEX 153

FORWARD

When I began this project, I wanted to create a study group and related study guide that would help weavers, including myself, create works of ART that were worthy of exhibition in national art museums and fine art galleries. When I presented the idea to my fellow guild members, I was surprised at the response. While most were excited about the possibilities, two of our most skilled weavers were offended by the suggestion that there was something wrong with their more functional weaving and were resistant to participating in the study group. Because both of them would be valuable members of the group, I stepped back and reevaluated what I really wanted to accomplish with the project and think about how I was presenting the overall concept.

As a teenager living south of Paris, I was fascinated with Impressionist painters. Where did their ideas come from? How did they influence each other? How did they see the world differently than the rest of us? As I got older, I preferred reading biographies and autobiographies of artists of all types, including musicians, actors, directors, dancers, and computer geniuses. I was always asking: How did they get to be so creative? Where did their ideas come from?

Throughout these years, I always felt that these Artists were different than me. I was an appreciator, a fan, a collector, but not an Artist. On the other hand, I have always been a maker. Whether it was dressmaking, knitting, quilting, weaving, or jewelry making, I usually followed other designer's patterns until I gained some proficiency and then started creating my own designs, with mixed results. Quilt making in the early 1990's was the first time I felt a freedom to express my ideas, and I learned that I could turn my mistakes into a final product much better than my original concept. I began to think that maybe I was an artist, but just not with a capital "A."

The possibility of exploring creativity for myself and with my group of weaving friends seemed like a natural extension of my life-long inquiry. And maybe I would then better understand what defines Art and the Artist. Very quickly, however, I realized how much those two words are in flux today. Some weavers are comfortable seeing themselves as craftsmen, true to the tradition, discipline, and tools of the weaver. Other weavers strive for an artistic identity, you see their original work and know who made it. Others enjoy the freedom of Saori weaving, relishing the immediacy of changing colors and textures as they go along, almost as if they were painting with oil.

The lines between what is Fine Art, High Craft, Functional Craft, and other permutations have been fought over for years. But where do handweavers fit in and what are our possibilities? I found the most reasonable definitions of creative makers in an *Atlantic Monthly* article by William Deresiewicz, entitled "The Death of the Artist—and the Birth of the Creative Entrepreneur," January 2015. He breaks makers into four general historical periods as follows:

Maker Term	Historical Period	Judge of Quality	Characteristics
Artisan	Before Late 18th Century	Patron	Followed tradition, discipline, and tools of the craft
Artist, Genius	Late 18th to mid 20th Century	Artists themselves	Rejected society, myth of solitary genius, part of movement, avoided "selling out," Avant-Garde, Art for Art's Sake
Professional Artist	Last half of 20th Century	Institutions and corporations	MFA, teaching at academia, able to explain what they were doing, climbed the ranks, fellowships
Creative Entrepreneur	Present	Customers	Network, sell directly to customers, multiple artistic identities, selling stressed in MFA programs, "No one has the right to tell us when our work is bad."

Innovative Weaving

Artists with a capital A don't have a place in this view of the present scene. In fact, I discovered that many creative people see that term as pretentious and, instead, identify themselves with their medium, such as painters, cartoonists, and photographers. As weavers, we can choose to be Creative Entrepreneurs or invent a new term for those of us who don't sell our work. How about Creative Artisans? But I am now comfortable simply being a weaver.

After this year of exploration within our study group, I am less interested in encouraging weavers to take on the Art World gatekeepers and am, instead, more motivated to help weavers enjoy the surprise and satisfaction of mining their own creativity, thus building their (and my own) confidence that we can create original work, work that expresses and celebrates our individuality. Whether it is "worthy" of a national art gallery is not relevant here. The subjective opinion of curators, exhibit judges, gallery owners, and even the marketplace, has no place in this book and resulting study groups. Maybe some day the arbiters of taste will catch up to our work and maybe not. But creating with those judgmental view points can be explored in some other effort.

INTRODUCTION

A weaver, like many other creative people, occupies a world where we are most appreciated by others of our craft. At a time when a weaver may spend several days in the process of making a dishtowel that can be bought at a big box store for a dollar, we may wonder how to produce work that has more aesthetic value than the cheap import, expressing an original and personal view of the world.

Innovative Weaving is intended for weavers and other makers who want to explore their own creativity in order to produce original work with intentional meaning. Like much contemporary art, beauty may or may not play a role. The assumption here is that inspiration for original work can be found when we step out of our specialty and look to the wide world of fine art and other creative endeavors, such as music and photography. While each chapter is focused on a specific art form, there are also relevant subthemes throughout that support our growth as weavers, such as collaboration, working in series, embracing failure, movement, and ensuring a legacy.

As a guide for conducting and participating in a creativity study group, each of *Innovative Weaving*'s chapters is intended to be covered within one monthly meeting. The Weavers and Spinners Society of Austin (WSSA) participated in a trial run through the twelve months of 2015. Thirty-six members received a chapter via email before each meeting. We had a core of about eight regular participants, and I facilitated. Meetings were held on a weekday afternoon in my Austin home.

Weavers and Spinners Society of Austin, Innovative Weaving study group, 2015.

Innovative Weaving

The study group format described here includes time for brainstorming, which provides an opportunity for participants to develop their own ideas and build on those of others, often helping us to push through any creative blocks we might have. Like our guilds' show-and-tell opportunities, the group provides motivation to complete a project by the next meeting. However most of us don't need more pressure on our time, thus ideas are more important here than finished projects.

While this book is structured to take advantage of the synergy within a study group, you will also benefit from the information and exercises presented here if, instead, you are working through the chapters alone. In the long term, the notebook you develop through the course will provide an ongoing source of inspiration, filled with new ideas, expanded designs, references, and inspirational images. Some of those ideas will be gems that can be further developed into original projects, whatever your medium.

Few things can be as thrilling as experiencing a spark of originality, whether it is a new way of solving a problem or a new way to visually present an idea. All of us members of WSSA hope that this book helps you have that experience many times over.

Innovative Weaving

MEETING ONE: GETTING STARTED WITH YOUR STUDY GROUP

This chapter provides guidelines for organizing a study group that will help you improve your ability to generate original ideas, thus expanding your creativity. It covers those organizational issues that are best agreed upon by the members during the first meeting, such as times and place, etc. If you are reading this book on your own, rather than as part of a study group, skip down to the Brainstorming section where idea generation is discussed.

In addition, this chapter explores some of the various approaches to creativity, including the definition of Open and Focused Creativity. A quiz helps you understand your own creative process preferences.

How to Organize Your Study Group

The following techniques are recommended to maximize the effectiveness of your study group.

Before the First Meeting

The study group organizer should send out an announcement before the first meeting that includes the information about the time, date, and location of the meeting, as well requesting that each member:

- Read this chapter up to the Exercises.
- Explore their creative past to remember the time when they felt most creative and what they made during that time that most pleased them. The exercise works best if people do not bring any examples. It is more about the experience, than the product.
- Bring a pen.

At the Beginning of the First Meeting

If everyone is not well acquainted with each other's name, take a few minutes at the beginning of the meeting to go around the room and state your name. The first exercise in this chapter provides further opportunity to get to know the other members of the group.

Creating an agreed upon organizational structure for your study group helps ensure the majority of your members attend the most meetings and enjoy expanding their creativity while there. Of course, there must be flexibility when circumstances change, but establishing agreed expectations of how the meetings are run creates a framework for the free flow of creative ideas to follow. In addition, agreement at the beginning of the group prevents valuable meeting time being wasted later on.

Consensus

If you find that the group needs to vote on some of the issues, consensus is an excellent method for ensuring that all members are in agreement. In consensus, a vote is taken with thumbs up for "Yes," thumbs down for "No," and a thumb to the side for "OK, but not thrilled." If there is a thumb down, the leader asks the dissenting member(s) how the vote statement might be modified to meet his or her concern. The decision is revised and another vote taken. This continues until the entire group is satisfied with the decision, shown by all thumbs up or to the side. Consensus doesn't mean everyone is happy with the final outcome, but everyone accepts it.

Organizational Issues Requiring Agreement

The following issues are best resolved before or at the first study group meeting. If a vote is needed, the following sections offer a possible statement for a consensus vote. However the vote statement should be revised and additional ones added to meet the needs of your study group.

- Who will lead the group?
- Will we have a minimum skill level?
- Will we have a minimum or maximum size?
- Will we close the membership after a specific date?
- When will we meet?
- Where will we meet?
- Should we plan refreshments?

Who Will Lead the Group?

One of the first tasks of your group is to agree upon who will lead all your meetings or if you are going to take turns. This person or persons might be called a "Leader," "Chairman," or "Facilitator." However the role of leading a creativity study group seems to be closer to the definition of Facilitator. Rather than leading a group toward a specific organizational goal, a Innovative Weaving Facilitator helps the participants reach their individual goals by ensuring that procedures are followed in order to maximize the creative inspiration of everyone, that each participant is able to share his or her ideas, and that the meeting time is used most effectively.

Some study groups may prefer to share the leadership role. The Facilitator could change every month as long as each person understands his or her individual responsibilities. During the meetings, the Facilitator is responsible for the following:

- Keeps the meeting moving effectively.
- Sensitively manages group dynamics.
- Ensures each person has an opportunity to speak.
- Presents a summary of the month's chapter.
- Manages the exercises, including controlling the amount of time spent on each.
- Provides opportunity for participants to share their designs, ideas, and projects inspired from previous meetings at the beginning of the meeting.
- Describes expected homework for the next.

Even if the leadership is to be shared, most groups benefit from having just one person tasked with reminding members of the date, time, place, and homework of the upcoming meetings.

Example Vote Statements

- We will take turns facilitating the meetings
- [Name of Facilitator] will lead the study group.

Meeting One: Getting Started with Your Study Group

Will We Have a Minimum Skill Level?

As in any creativity endeavor, the *Open Your Weaving* study group benefits from diversity in its members. Beginner weavers will spark ideas in advanced weavers as much as the opposite. In addition, all levels of knitters, dyers, and spinners will bring fresh ideas to the table, as will members that have no textile skills. This journey is about fresh ideas, and the more diverse the group the more exciting ideas will emerge.

Example Vote Statements

- We welcome any person no matter their skills.
- We welcome any weaver no matter their skill level.
- We welcome any fiber artist no matter their skill level.

How Many People Will We Allow in the Group?

Optimum size for an *Innovative Weaving* study group is from 6-10 people at each meeting. Certainly the size of the planned meeting space will affect the optimum number of people in the group. While a smaller group will provide more time for each person to share their ideas, more people will have a wider range of diverse ideas. At some point, a larger group may find that it works best to break into two parts for some exercises and then come together to report out consolidated results.

Example Vote Statements

- We will cap the regular membership at 15 people.
- We will set no limit to the number of members.
- Will We Close the Membership After a Specific Date?

A creativity study group benefits from having membership closed after the first meeting. If all goes well, every group eventually settles into a comfortable and supportive atmosphere during their meetings. A new member joining in the middle potentially can disrupt that dynamic. However, if the group votes to allow open membership, the new person should be required to read all the *Innovative Weaving* chapters he or she has missed.

Example Vote Statements

- We will close membership to new members before the second meeting.
- We will allow members to join the group at any time.

When Will We Meet?

A regular schedule of meetings avoids confusion and allows members to plan far ahead. Once a month gives people time to develop designs and to weave projects, and a set end date for getting through the book helps keep the group progressing at a reasonable pace.

Example Vote Statement

- We will meet on the second Wednesday of the month at 7:00 pm for the next 12 months.

Innovative Weaving

Where Will We Meet?

Ideally all the members are able to sit around a table where they can see each other and have a comfortable surface to write on. For larger groups, a circle of chairs will do.

Also it would be good to have the meetings at the same location each month. However having members take turns hosting the meeting will have its benefits, such as giving them an opportunity to see each other's studios. Just be sure to allow time for the tour.

Example Vote Statements

- We will meet every month at [location].
- We will take turns hosting the meeting.

Should We Plan Refreshments?

If refreshments are a requirement for your meetings, a sign-up sheet can spread the responsibility for bringing refreshments and allow people to plan ahead. Encouraging that the refreshments somehow relate to the theme of the meeting can add to the creative atmosphere. The connection might be obvious or more of a wordplay, such as a pun that requires the group to guess the connection to the theme.

Example Vote Statements

- The member hosting the meeting at his or her home will provide light refreshments.
- We will not have refreshments at our meetings.
- We will each sign up to bring refreshments for at least one meeting.

Meeting Agenda

Even retirees find that they continue to have a busy schedule and grow impatient with meetings that go on too long. That impatience is stronger in those working full time and with a family to tend to. Thus managing the length of the study group meetings is one of the most important challenges. How can your group maximize the creativity of the individual members, make sure everyone has the benefit of hearing each other's ideas, and yet keep the meetings to a reasonable length? The following is a possible agenda for a meeting two hours long. An explanation of each item follows.

SAMPLE AGENDA

    A. Sharing designs, samples, and final projects from previous meetings (25 minutes)
    B. Summary of month's *Innovative Weaving* chapter (15 minutes)
    C. Exercise 1 (30 minutes)
    D. Exercise 2 (30 minutes)
    E. Homework for Next Meeting (5 minutes)
    F. Evaluate Meeting (15 minutes)

A. Sharing Designs, Samples, and Final Projects

The whole group benefits when each of you shares what you have accomplished during the month, whether it is additional ideas, designs, a few samples, or even a finished project. Your skill level is immaterial, neither is the medium you used. If you created something inspired by the study group, your work will be celebrated, whether it is perfect or turned out to be a failure in your eyes. The group will learn from it.

B. Summary of Month's Chapter

The Facilitator should create a concise summary of the chapter to present at the meeting, allowing time for questions and discussion. The summary should include those points that will be most helpful for the exercises and are most relevant to the interests of the group. When the members read the chapter in advance, a complete overview shouldn't be necessary.

C and D. Exercises

The exercises usually involve silent brainstorming as described later in this chapter, followed by a time to share some of the ideas each individual has written down. This sharing is best implemented by going around the room, one person speaking at a time, with others simply listening or asking questions. Members are encouraged to build on each other's ideas and to write down anything that strikes them during the sharing.

E. Homework for Next Month's Meeting

The Facilitator should remind the members about any homework they should do before the next meeting, such as further developing their ideas through the coming month, reading the next chapter, and any other preparation listed at the end of the chapter.

F. Evaluate Meeting

At the end of each meeting, it is most helpful if the group takes time to evaluate what worked well and what could be changed. Depending upon the group, this can either be in written form, or verbal, if everyone is comfortable enough with each other. People are going to be anxious to leave, so this should be accomplished quickly, while the Facilitator notes the group's suggestions.

Member Responsibilities

The responsibilities of the Facilitator already have been detailed, but the members of the study group also have responsibilities necessary to ensure the group runs smoothly and effectively. Each member of the study group is encouraged to:

- Read the relevant *Innovative Weaving* chapter before each meeting, exclusive of the exercises.
- Be sensitive to the times the discussion is going around the room, one person speaking at a time, and when it is a more freewheeling discussion.
- Bring refreshments when it is your turn, if appropriate.
- Be aware what the homework assignment is and complete as much as you are able.
- Share what you have accomplished, even if it is less than you would like or not the quality you would like.
- Follow the brainstorming rules as described next.

Brainstorming

Brainstorming, the core of an *Innovative Weaving* study group, is the process of silently and individually generating as many ideas as possible, based upon some sort of problem or prompt, sharing a few of these ideas with the group, and then building on your own and each other's ideas.

Innovative Weaving

In this study group, brainstorming exercises will use various forms of art to inspire members to develop ideas for weaving projects. These concepts can be used both in your study group and when you are working alone. At the next meeting you will use painting for inspiration, followed by sculpture and other art forms. After the meeting, you are encouraged to develop these ideas into one or two designs, samples, or possibly a final project that you can share at a subsequent meeting.

In order to generate the maximum number of ideas with a few gems, you must prevent yourselves from judging too quickly. It is natural for most of us to think that an unusual or unexpected idea is silly or impractical. However on the other side might be something that can be developed into an inspired original work. Thus you need to dump your brain of all the more usual and practical ideas and get to those that you wouldn't think of as long as you wear a judge's hat. The more you dump, the closer you get to the fresh, inventive ideas.

When you are in a brainstorming exercise, everyone must remember the following rules to maximize the number of ideas generated

- Remain silent during the brainstorming writing time
- No criticizing or judging of your own or other's ideas
- Create as many ideas as possible in the time allotted
- Write down each idea in short phrases, rather than paragraphs.
- Write down the ideas as they come
- Share a few of the ones that excite you the most during the sharing time
- Write down any ideas that are sparked by someone else's ideas during the share

Inspiration Notebook

The *Innovative Weaving* study group is intended to generate ideas you can use after the meeting and into the longer future. In order to preserve this mine of creative ideas, you need to collect them somehow. During the year of the study group, you will be generating and receiving the following:

- Creativity Style Quiz
- Creativity Goals
- Brainstormed ideas each month
- References to books, periodicals, and websites
- Inspirational images from magazines, web, etc.
- Your designs
- Your drawdowns, either hand drawn or computer generated
- Your photos of samples and final projects, both your own and others
- Samples
- Additional handouts

What method you use to collect and manage all these items is less important than that you do it. You will often want to use your notebook for inspiration in the future, thus you want it to be easily accessible and in one place. A loose-leaf notebook will work well, with a tab for each month's meeting. But so will using your laptop or tablet, as long as you bring it to every meeting and have the applications that will best organize the material.

Meeting One: Getting Started with Your Study Group

Creativity Definitions

We all create every day, even if it is simply transforming fresh bread into a piece of toast. But some of you are driven to pull together raw materials and make something you can wear, use, or simply display. Some of you will believe it is only good if it looks just like something else you have seen, while others will only believe it is good if it looks different than everyone else's. Such a judgment is made upon the product itself. However, in this book we do not pass judgment on our work to decide if it is "good" or not. Such analysis would only hamper the free flow of ideas.

On the other hand, understanding the value of originality is worthwhile. The author of *Zen and the Art of Motorcycle Maintenance*, Robert Persig, explores the advantages of both tradition and innovation in his 1991 book, *Lila*, where he defines "Static" and "Dynamic" quality. He says Static Quality is excellence that conforms to the "established pattern of fixed values." When we follow a pattern to a "t" and are happy with the results, we have achieved Static Quality. An example, Figure 1.1 is a practice piece for a young Balinese girl learning how to dye traditional double ikat, which she then wove on a backstrap loom in loose plain weave. She will eventually master the sacred technique as required in her community's Hindu rituals.

Figure 1.1. Practice piece of Geringsing, double ikat, plain weave. Cotton, natural dyes. Tenganan Pegeringsingan, Bali, 2010.

Persig defines Dynamic Quality as excellence that "comes as a sort of surprise," "cutting edge," and "always new." We know it when we see it, such as Molly Koehn's piece below. In *Shuttle Spindle & Dyepot* Fall 2015, the graduate student describes her fascination with a post-apocalyptic world, "I think the idea of nature taking over the earth is really beautiful." She used rusty metal to stain her white cotton handweaving for *Invasion*, and then embroidered maggots, known as nature's recyclers, on the surface.

Figure 1.2. Molly Koehn, *Invasion*, 2015. Hand-woven cotton, embroidery floss, rust dye. 12 x 18 in. Photo courtesy of artist.

Both types of quality are essential for advancement in science, technology, government, culture, and art. Dynamic Quality pushes the limits, while Static Quality insures the "pattern" is written down and repeatable. Static Quality is evident in the popularity of weaving Early American coverlets and linens from old drawdowns using authentic yarns and natural dyes. On the other hand, starting in the late 1960's and early 1970's, weavers began experimenting with unusual undyed yarns, dimension, and structure. That whole era was about Dynamic Quality. The unexpected was expected.

Aurèlia Muñoz (Spain, 1926-2011) was one of the early artists to revive the old technique of macramé. Her *Capas* series was inspired by Mexican rainwear. Using coarse sisal, she experimented with gravity, negative space, dimension, and the vertical and horizontal.

Figure 1.3. Aurèlia Muñoz. *Capa pluvial II*, 1976. Sisal, 200 x 25 cm. Fondation Toms Pauli, Lausanne, Switzerland (photo AN Lausanne Arnaud Conne)

Persig's approach explores the results of creativity, while the Right-Brained versus Left-Brained model, popularized by Betty Edward's 1979 book, *Drawing on the Right Side of the Brain*, explores the source of creativity, the maker's mind. The right side of the brain is said to be the source of intuition and is subjective, while the left side is more logical and objective. While this theory explains our experience with different types of professionals, such as artists vs dentists, scientists find this theory an over-simplification and, in fact, wrong. They see the brain as far more complex.

On the other hand, we do find that most people clearly have a preference for one creative style over the other. These can be called Open and Focused. Those who prefer the Open Creativity style are always searching for new ways to express themselves, new ways to push the limits of their art, whatever that might be. Those who prefer a more Focused Creativity style are less concerned with innovation and more concerned with good craftsmanship and the commonly held understanding of what "good" means.

On the other hand, in order to create anything, we must use both styles during the process of making. Sometimes you will be deep in the Open style, other times completely Focused. In your study group meetings, you will exercise Open Creativity during brainstorming, attempting to pull up as many original ideas as you can. But when you go home and try to make sense of all of those ideas, you will put on your Focused Creativity hat and sort through what is actually possible to do. You will begin the process of translating those cutting edge ideas into something you can actually produce with the skills, supplies, and equipment you have. There will be times during this Focused process, when you will need to go to your Open Creativity, such as when you find you don't have the color of yarn you need in your stash or realize the planned structure is impractical and you need to go into a problem-solving mode. But in order to wind the warp, dress the loom, and throw the shuttle time after time after time, you have to go back to the exactness of the Focused mind.

Meeting One: Getting Started with Your Study Group

Exercises

The following exercises will help you understand your own individual approach to creativity.

Exercise 1.1 (30 minutes)

Like all the exercises in this book, sit in a circle of chairs or around a table. Going around the room one at a time, tell the group about a time in your life when you felt most creative and what you made during that time that most pleased you.

Exercise 1.2 (30 minutes)

The Creativity Preference Quiz will help you examine your own creative process and then help you decide if you want to create more of a balance.

Creativity Preference Quiz

Circle the answer that is closer to how you would respond to each situation. Likely none are exactly what you would do, just answer with what comes closest to your reaction.

1		You committed to submit some new work for a guild show six months away. How do you proceed?
	a	Within a couple of weeks after the commitment, I decide what I want to submit, begin the design process, and order the yarn. I plan to get my piece in a week before the deadline.
	b	I start considering the possibilities right away, but it isn't until a couple of weeks before the show that I settle on what I want to weave. I often just barely made the deadline, but people really love the results.
2		You are taking a weaving class on a technique that is completely new to you.
	a	I take notes in class, but felt frustrated that the instructor didn't pass out a thorough handout that I can refer to after the class.
	b	I am most interested in getting the gist of the technique. There will be someone to ask if I have problems in the future. It's just nice to be in class with people I like.
3		You just bought a new weaving tool, but it isn't obvious how to use it.
	a	Rather than ask the vendor where I bought it, I count on the instructions and pull them out when it is time to actually use the tool.
	b	I spend quite a while with the vendor, watching how to use the tool, asking questions, and just talking about the conference. Oh, there are instructions?
4		You want to buy a new loom. How do you make the decision?
	a	I go through my weaving magazines and online for recent reviews. I make a chart of the advantages and disadvantages of the models and manufacturers.
	b	I saw a loom at a conference and it was sooo beautiful and it felt so good to weave on. I liked the salesperson. But then I might get a new wheel instead.
5		You have been working for a while on a project that is coming to an end.
	a	I am eager to finish it, add a swatch and drawdown to the documentation, and mail the project off. At times I wish I had made it more original.
	b	I sometimes have trouble finishing a project because I keep thinking of cool ways I can improve it, plus I've got quite a few other projects that I'm working on at the same time.

Innovative Weaving

6		Your guild president has asked you to help rewrite the bylaws.
	a	I jump on the chance to work through the language and policy details. I am eager to make those corrections that have been bothering me for some time.
	b	Why do we need bylaws?
7		You are asked to make another baby blanket just like the one you made for your sister, but this time in blue. How do you proceed?
	a	I pull out the drawdown and notes from the first one that documented the yarn I used, sett, size, etc.
	b	I hate making the same thing twice, plus I never keep any documentation. But I've got a few cool ideas I'm sure my sister will like even more.
8		The guild president asks you to chair an upcoming fashion show?
	a	I need to know how things were done last year. Who did the sound? Where are the entry forms and rules?
	b	I see this as a great opportunity to make the fashion show more fun and inclusive. I already have ideas for the music and announcer.

Scoring

Count up the number of "a"s and "b"s. Are they evenly divided or do you favor one or the other?

Focused Creativity

If you have significantly more "a"s, then you have a preference for a process using Focused Creativity. You more often meet deadlines and can repeat successful projects due to your good documentation. You are known for your organizational skills and your craftsmanship. Your work expresses Static Quality.

The disadvantage of a more Focused Creativity is that you might not have the originality and flexibility you would like. If you yearn to tap into your own originality and possibly creating something possibly a bit "wacky," the brainstorming in this book may help you pull those ideas out of your experience and imagination.

Open Creativity

If you have significantly more "b"s, than you prefer the Open creative process. Original ideas come more easily for you. You are less likely to be boxed in by what others might think of your work. You spend time generating and sorting through ideas, with little time or desire to document what you do. Your work likely expresses Dynamic Quality.

On the other hand, you likely have so many projects going on at once that you may find yourself overwhelmed. You may have little patience for some of the more repetitive aspects of weaving. Your lack of focus may make meeting deadlines a continual struggle. You may be unable to repeat a project, due to lack of documentation and simply a lack of will, despite the promise of a sizable commission.

Flexibility

In order to create our most satisfying work, we need to use both Open and Focused creative skills. Open Creativity is needed in much of the design process and for problem solving. We need to be "Available," ready for inspiration that can be found all around us. If you don't see it where you are, go for a walk, meditate, or go to the library. The answers are waiting for you.

Meeting One: Getting Started with Your Study Group

But we need more than ideas to actually create something. We need to implement them and that only comes when we use Focused Creativity. Both the "drudgery" and the meditative qualities of weaving happen when we are focused. Putting our initial design into weaving software, winding the warp, threading the heddles, and the actual throwing of the shuttle all require us to have the patience and exactness of Focused Creativity.

However, during Innovative Weaving study group meetings, you will be exercising your Open Creativity skills. Homework will provide the opportunity to practice your Focused Creativity chops.

Exercise 1.3 (15 minutes)

Going around the room one at a time answer the following question:

1. Are you comfortable with the results of your Creativity Quiz? Yes or No
2. What are the areas of your creative process that you would like to work on for the next year?

_____

_____

Conclusion

In this chapter you have agreed upon the organizational structure of the study group, learned about brainstorming, and explored your own style of creativity.

For the Next Meeting

- Write down any inspiration that comes your way in the next month in your notebook.
- Find a loose-leaf notebook or style of journal that will work for your inspiration notebook, whether hard copy or computerized, and bring it to the next meeting.
- Read the next chapter on Painting, exclusive of the exercises.

Innovative Weaving

MEETING TWO: PICTURE IT ON YOUR LOOM

In this chapter, we explore the fine art of painting as inspiration for your weaving. A painter with brush in hand may seem worlds away from a weaver at the loom, but the two creative acts are more similar than you may first think. Any formal study of painting, like that of weaving, includes the vocabulary of design and color. The materials and technical execution may be different, but the Open Creativity process is similar. Thus when we look at a successful painting and consider the artist's many decisions, we open channels to our own creativity.

Painting as Inspiration

The process of creating a painted picture has an immediacy not to be found in the weaver's world. When applying oil to canvas, decisions can be made quickly and are often easily corrected. The painter's ability to be in the moment has lead to more experimentation, particularly in the 20th Century, than is possible in the world of handweaving. Of course, weavers experiment, but we will naturally be a little more cautious to change course in the middle of a work, considering the hours and money invested in warping the loom. It is much more challenging to reuse warp than it is to reuse a canvas.

We choose to weave, rather than paint, because we enjoy the meditative rhythm of throwing the shuttle and the primal pleasure of feeling yarn in our hands. Some of us find the repetitive exactness of threading heddles as satisfying, while others may merely tolerate the task. When we weave, rather than paint, we best embrace the challenge of the inherent geometry of the warp and weft, along with all the necessary calculations. But the one benefit that weavers have over painting is that we have the option to create a piece that we can caress and that can enfold our loved ones, rather than merely hanging on the wall.

Despite the different technical skills required for painting and weaving, the elements of design, such as color, value, and texture, are the same. By paying attention to each of those aspects of a painting, you are giving yourself the opportunity to bring something new to your own work. Consider the following:

Dimension

By definition, a painting, like most weaving, has essentially two dimensions with a length and a width. When you look at a painting, consider the proportion of these two outer measurements. Did the artist play with the standard rectangle? How does the overall size of the piece affect its significance?

Notice the effect of the frame and how it not only protects the work, but adds to its sense of importance. The relative size of the frame and its decorative style can give you an idea on how you might frame your own work, either with an actual wood or metal frame for the wall or create a border around a functional weaving, such as a table runner. Contemporary paintings are often not surrounded by a separate frame. In those cases, how does the painter handle the edges? The painter may have made aesthetic choices that present possibilities for your own work.

Innovative Weaving

Shape

Before painters dab on the first spot of color, they usually decide whether they will attempt to make realistic images, distort them a little, create abstractions of reality, or completely avoid recognizable imagery. The painter is not bound by the loom's grid of warp and weft. While tapestry, the drawloom, and jacquard weaving provide the ability to create somewhat realistic images, many of us weavers enjoy the challenge of fitting our ideas into the grid, not unlike how some modernist painters did early in the 20th Century. The rigidity of the warp and weft provides both a limitation and a gift. Overshot, summer and winter, and double weave are only some of the possible structures that provide opportunities for playing with abstracted shapes.

When you look at a painting, observe how shapes are placed in relationship to each other and what their sizes are relative to each other. What in the painting excites you and invites you to interpret the shapes into your own work?

Texture

When a painter selects the medium to use, such as oil, watercolor, casein, tempura, or acrylic, she or he is deciding on the texture to use to cover the canvas, since each type of paint has its own textural characteristics. As you look at a painting, notice whether the paint was put on thickly or watered down. Were other materials, such as sand or other thickener, added to raise the surface? Where does the painter create surface contrast between smooth and rougher areas?

Physical texture is where weavers have at least as much flexibility as a painter, particularly with the wide range of yarns available today, including those you can spin yourself. In addition, the ability to manipulate sett and structure, such as the difference between smooth satin and thick-and-thin collapsed weaves, provides the opportunity to vary the texture within a piece.

Texture for a weaver requires other decisions unnecessary for an artist smearing paint on a plain-weave canvas stretched on a rigid frame. Consideration of the appropriate drape is essential for a successful woven piece. Will it hang stiffly on a wall or will it need to fall around a human body in soft folds? Selecting the appropriate sett, structure, and technique are textural decisions specific to the weaver.

Two paintings by contemporary artist Lynn Putney (American, b. 1963) were used for inspiration at the second meeting of the Weavers and Spinners of Austin's Innovative Weaving study group. A small reproduction of her *I Put This Moment (Here)*, shown in the top left of Figure 2.1, provided WSSA guild member Sandra Doak the inspiration for a shawl, still on the loom in the photo. The high-relief black loops reflect the loops in the painting. Turquoise and black inlaid wefts provide even more texture.

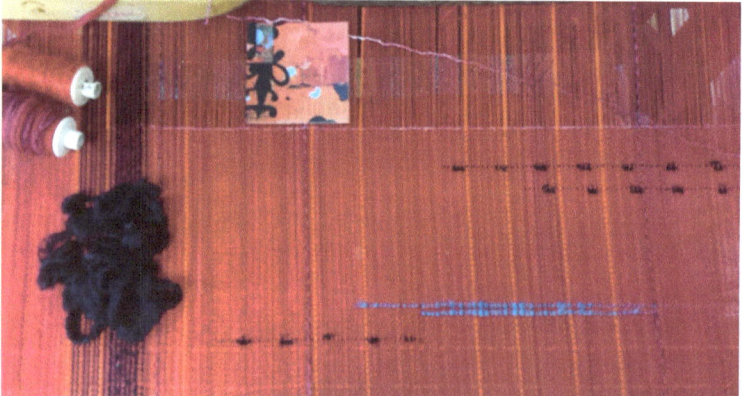

Figure 2.1 Sandra Doak, *Red Cloud*. Shawl. 2015. Wool, silk, and other fibers. Courtesy of the artist.

Meeting Two: Picture It on Your Loom

Line

Analyzing how painters use lines might be one of the more important lessons for weavers. After all, weaving is composed of the intersections of horizontal and vertical lines. But which ones do you want to call attention to and which ones do you want to fall into the background?

Painters will often use a darker line around those objects they want to stand out. A line will direct your eye where the painter wants you to focus your attention. And the straight lines of the enclosing frame make clear the limits of the painting.

Paintings provide examples of how to balance and control lines to create the mood you are intending. Granted, painters have more freedom on their surface to incorporate curves and changes in color, such as we find in *Good Day, Sunshine* by Lynn Putney. In addition to her play with line, notice her bold use of color blocks, division of space, and play of the same color on different backgrounds. How might you incorporate these ideas into a weaving, despite the limitations of warp and weft?

Figure 2.2. Lynn Putney, *Good Day Sunshine*, 2013. Casein.

Color

Paintings can also inspire your use of color. A successful painting must show complete control of the color choices, even if it is a seemingly improvisational work such as one by Jackson Pollack. Some colors will attract you more than others, possibly providing combinations you might not have considered before. The earthy tones of Cezanne might do the trick for you, while someone else might appreciate the pastels of Monet more. Be sure to take advantage of every opportunity to see a painting up close in order to analyze an artist's decisions, particularly those that are too subtle to see in a photograph.

Figure 2.3. Georges Lemmen, *Beach at Heist*, 1891. Oil on Wood. 14.8 x 18 in. Courtesy Musée d'Orsay, Paris.

The school of painting begun by Georges Seurat (French, 1859-1891), now called Neo-Impressionism, Pointillism, or Divisionism, provides an opportunity for you to explore color choices for your warp and weft in a new way. Seurat, as well as Georges Lemmen (Belgian, 1865-1916), used dots and dashes of pure color to

Innovative Weaving

make other colors as seen from a distance. The Neo-Impressionists avoided black and earth tone paints, attempting to bring luminosity to their work.

Look closely at *Beach at Heist* by Georges Lemmen and you can see how he combined colors, created denser areas of color, contrast, space, all with dots and dabs. The palette of painted and dyed yarns give weavers the opportunity to create similar complexity, particularly if you dye your warp and weft specifically for a piece.

Iridescence, with the cross between one color of warp and just the right contrasting color of weft, is a way a weaver can play with dots of color. Bobbie Irwin has written several articles about the iridescent effect of shiny split complements in a balanced weave. Dots, formed by the crossing of different colors in the warp and weft, such as a blue-green weft and an orange and red warp, cause different hues to dominant depending on how they catch the light.

The wide color choices of commercially dyed yarns available today provide you an enormous palette. On the other hand, hand-dyeing techniques such as painted warps and ikat provide limitless possibilities for your own interpretation of the colors inspired by a painting. Workshops, such as those taught by Carol Soderlund at Pro-Chemical and Dye, in Fall River, Massachusetts, can teach you to combine the three primaries of yellow, blue, and red into an endless variety of colors to work into your weaving. By dyeing multiple hues spaced along a skein of weft and wound warp, you can create all the variety found in a Pointillist painting.

Figure 2.4. Mickey Stam, Runner, 2012. Hand-dyed, handwoven cotton.

Value

You can also learn how to create more interest in your work by observing how painters use shadows and contrasts in light and dark. Some weavers struggle with the effective use of the right balance of different values, causing their work to appear flat or too busy. While we might blame the color choices, it might actually be the value that is the problem. How has the painter used lighter and darker colors to make the important areas stand out? Variations in the values of even one color will create a piece of much more interest. Careful placement of a few darker and lighter warp ends may be all you need to make a weaving appear more intriguing.

Content

While we quickly notice the colors, shapes, and different values in a painting, its full content may be more elusive. Even if a story seems clear at first, the artist's intention may not be so obvious. Painters are often driven to paint so that they can make some sort of statement, possibly personal, political, or social. When you look at a painting, consider if there is a message that touches you in some way and even inspires ideas for your own work.

Meeting Two: Picture It on Your Loom

Is there something you would like to say through a piece, whether the viewer will understand it or not? Your intention might be obvious, defined in the title, written in your artist statement, or simply used to inspire the work and kept close to your chest. Many artists find that by not attaching a specific meaning to their work, viewers are more intrigued and often connect with their own story. Are there specific painters that speak to you? Is content important to them? If so, how do they communicate that content?

Developing content in your work requires you to be in the Open Creativity mode. What parts of yourself can you put into a piece? What experience have you had that you would like to share in some way? What do you care most deeply about?

Style

Despite all attempts by a painter or any other creative person to be completely original, they will still end up working within a set of standards or expectations set by other artists, patrons, customers, critics, gallery owners, teachers, parents, and friends. The artist may continually rebel against these expectations, but very rare is any work completely free of some basic expectations, self-imposed or not. If a painting appears unbound by any well-known style, experts may label it Outsider Art, which includes work by self-taught painters not influenced by art schools or folk art traditions.

Whether the standards are documented by a group of other artists, such as Impressionists or Cubists, rebelling against the establishment, or academics and critics attempting to categorize artists by their similarities, the definition of the style helps us understand the standards the painter used to both confine and push their work.

Consider the style of a painting, when it was painted, and how that influenced the painter's choices. What are the characteristics of that style and can it inform your own work? Or are you more drawn to rebel against that style and go in the opposite direction?

Weavers also have their own expectations, standards, and styles. Even those of us who didn't go to art school are influenced by the books and magazines we read, the classes we take, and our fellow guild members. Therefore you may find it reassuring to realize that complete "originality" is rare, if not impossible.

Saori, a contemporary weaving style developed in Japan by Misao Jo in 1968, uses plain weave and encourages dynamic quality through personal expression, with a spontaneous use of textured and colored wefts, with less focus on the exactitude of straight selvedges and an even beat. As a counterpoint to Saori, static quality is important when working toward the Handweavers Guild of America's Certificate of Excellence (COE). HGA judges will deduct points for uncontrolled selvedges and an uneven beat. While each applicant brings his or her own aesthetic, the COE requirements can also be considered a style or standard of weaving.

Like a painter, you have the freedom to originate your own set of standards to work within or you can select a style that meets your personal aesthetic and use it as a jumping off point for your own creativity. But before you settle on your own style, you might want to spend some time researching some painters and styles that you don't immediately like. Exploring art without judgment might introduce you to ideas you can incorporate into your own work.

Innovative Weaving

Generating Ideas through Open Creativity

During the second study group meeting, you will practice using brainstorming techniques by studying two different paintings in this chapter, one over 100 years old and the other contemporary. As you look at each painting, consider what aspects of it you might use in your own work. Don't judge whether the ideas are doable. You should be using only your Open Creativity skills for brainstorming. In your studio, you will practice your Focused Creativity skills to sift through the ideas you've generated during the exercises for ones that you can actually develop into a woven piece.

If you allow yourself to be open and available to possibilities, ideas will begin to flow. Write each one down in your Inspiration notebook, using a phrase just long enough to remember the idea. You can also make quick sketches, if an idea comes that way. You might feel an affinity to the example painting or you might be inspired to go against the work and attempt something quite different. All is good. It is also possible that an idea seemingly unrelated will pop up, write it down. You may also find yourself thinking of a medium other than weaving, write it down. As Maharishi Mahesh Yogi told John Lennon when he asked what he should do if a song came to him while meditating, "Write it down."

Whatever you do, don't let yourself get stuck trying to decide if you should write something down or not. Better to get it out and let it go, than let a questionable idea jam up the works. No judging at this point.

Brainstorming Guidelines

During the brainstorming exercises follow these guidelines to ensure the experience is most valuable for you and your follow study group members:

- Remain silent
- No criticizing or judging
- Write as many ideas as possible
- Use short phrases

After the defined time period for brainstorming, take turns going around the room and share two or three of the ideas that excite you the most from your notebook. Don't worry about what the group might think. Feel free to jot down ideas that come to you during the sharing. You don't want to lose any gem. By ensuring you capture the thought in your notebook, you can listen to what others have to say and thus remain open to even more ideas.

Exercises

The following exercises provide opportunities to study a couple of paintings and develop ideas you can incorporate into your weaving.

Exercise 2.1 (30 minutes)

Ten Minutes Study *Beach at Heist* by Georges Lemmen (Figure 2.3) in this chapter. Note how certain colors, such as blue, appear throughout. How might you use warp and weft in pure colors to create new colors? What else do you see in the painting that you could use in your own work, such as contrasting value? Sketch or write down as many ideas as you can in your notebook.

Meeting Two: Picture It on Your Loom

Twenty Minutes One at a time, share two or three of your ideas with the group and note any subsequent ideas that come to mind.

Exercise 2.2 (30 minutes)

Ten Minutes Study *Good Day, Sunshine* by Lynn Putney (Figure 2.2) in this chapter. Note the division of space, the movement, repetition of colors, effect of the colors on different backgrounds. How might you use these ideas in your work? Consider the other questions earlier in the chapter. Sketch or write as many ideas as you can in your notebook.

Twenty Minutes One at a time, share two or three of your ideas with the group and note any subsequent ideas that come to mind.

Conclusion

Paintings provide a vast and continually expanding wealth of inspiration for the weaver. When you use your Open Creativity skills to explore the choices that a painter made to express ideas, you open your mind to original ideas for your own work. Through brainstorming in your study group, a trip to the library for art books, or a visit to an art museum, opening your mind to the creativity of others can only help you expand your own inventiveness.

Further Resources for Inspiration

The Metropolitan Museum of Art www.metmuseum.org/collection/the-collection-online

Google Art Project www.google.com/culturalinstitute/project/art-project

Before the Next Meeting

After each meeting, review your ideas with a more critical eye. Use your Focused Creativity skills to select one or two ideas to develop.

- Look through all the ideas you generated in your Inspiration notebook.
- Circle a few that excite you the most.
- Decide on one that you would like to develop.
- Expand on the idea in your notebook, as you have time, with further drawings, drawdown, yarn calculations, yarn selections, etc.
- If you get stuck, note down where the problems are, such as: missing skills, material, or equipment. The great idea might have to wait until you have all you need.
- If possible, complete the project.

Read the next chapter.

Bring to the Next Meeting

Whether you are a beginner or a master weaver, everyone in the group benefits when you share your work. So as you head out to each study group meeting, remember to bring the following:

- A developed design, project in progress, or a finished piece inspired by this or a previous chapter.
- Your Inspiration notebook.

Innovative Weaving

MEETING THREE: TRIAL AND ERROR IN THREE DIMENSIONS

During the third study group meeting, we explore the three-dimensional art of sculpture, which provides innovative possibilities for your weaving. Some of you might take up the challenge to create a free-standing piece using your loom-woven fabric, such as this quadruple weave by WSSA member Sandy Curtis or develop a sculptural relief that hangs on the wall. This chapter might encourage you to also explore ideas for adding three-dimensional texture to your work by using different materials, weave structures, or patterns.

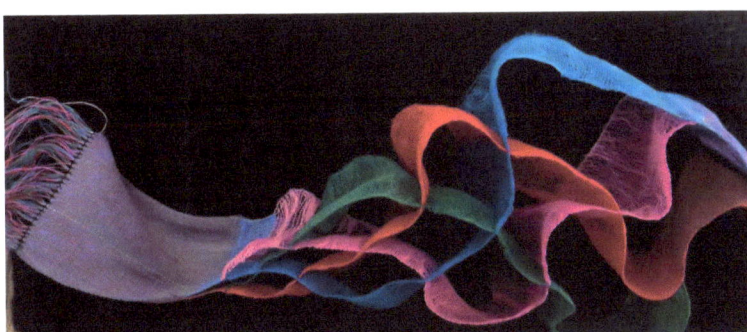

Figure 3.1. Sandy Curtis, *Phish*. 1994. Quadruple weave, cotton sewing thread. 13 x 5.5 x 3 inches.

Whichever course you take, you may be stepping into areas not yet explored by other weavers. Thus you may come up with a great idea, but have no idea how to implement it. Almost every original idea requires original methods for bringing it to fruition. Therefore, in this chapter, we address the importance of prototyping and sampling while developing the patience and persistence to making your vision come to life. The results may not necessarily end up how you first envisioned, but through the process of switching between Open and Focused Creativity, the final product will likely be even better than you first imagined.

A Very Brief History of Sculpture

People have been recreating the human figure in the round for over 40,000 years. Throughout the world, people have molded and carved representations of people, animals, and mythical creatures, using whatever materials and technologies were available. Most of this work has decayed over time, however stone and metal sculptures have survived from many cultures all over the world. Materials may have changed, but the subjects were most often the human figure, animals, and anthropomorphic creatures.

While it is definitely a valuable experience to learn about sculpture before the 20th Century, it is the works of Modernism that may have the most relevance to weavers. Pablo Picasso (Spanish, 1881-1973) is said to have first inspired the movement with his three-dimensional abstracted constructions of scrap lumber in 1913, which challenged the need for precious materials and realistic images. Then in 1917, Marcel Duchamp (French, 1887-1968) thumbed his nose at the adoration of Art with his common, "ready-made" urinal, entitled *Fountain*. His gesture questioned why anything couldn't be stripped of its original meaning and then be declared Art. The further move to abstracted sculpture is attributed to Constantin Brâncuși (Romanian, 1876-1957), who attempted to represent only the essence of a subject, leaving out all the unnecessary detail.

Modernism became the overarching term for all the sculptural styles that followed, such as Cubism, Geometric Abstraction, Pop-Art, Minimalism, Installation Art, and Public Art. (Installation Art will be explored in Meeting 12, and Public Art in Meeting 10.) Since we can't adequately cover all these styles here, you are encouraged to explore them on your own.

Innovative Weaving

By mid-20th Century, sculpture seemed to have reached a state of "no holds barred." Any material and any subject could now be considered sculpture, whether free-standing, relief against a wall, or suspended, as long as it had three dimensions. The restriction to marble and bronze as the only viable material for serious sculpture went out the door when Modernism came in. Welding steel in the studio became possible with advancements in technology after WWII. While some sculptors continued to use the more long lasting materials, others explored the more ephemeral medium of textiles. By the 1960s, weavers were making large Modernist sculptural wall hangings with silk, wool, cotton, and other materials that didn't need to have figural content or a subject matter other than a celebration of the manipulation of the warp and weft.

Of all the 40,000 years of sculpture, the last one hundred have been the most exhilarating, possibly because there appears to be more spontaneity or possibly because sculpture no longer requires a wealthy sponsor to pay for expensive materials and skilled support staff. Certainly those resources continue to be needed for a monumental piece, and expensive materials and well-developed skills are still highly valued, but now anyone can create a sculpture. Whether it is "successful" or not is another issue.

Applying Sculptural Elements to Weaving

The following elements are used in the analysis of sculpture as an art form. But they can also help us weavers reconsider possibilities for our own work. How much of the third dimension you incorporate into your weaving is up your own aesthetic, skills, and imagination. But developing the eye of the sculptor and understanding the following sculptural elements can only help ensure the effectiveness of your work.

Viewing Angle

360 Degrees

Figure 3.2 Charles Umlauf, *Family* [detail from back of sculpture], 1960, bronze. UMLAUF Sculpture Garden & Museum, Austin, Texas.

Free-standing sculpture is intended to be seen by walking completely around it. There may be an intended front, but interest continues from all angles. For example, in *The Family* by Charles Umlauf (American, 1910-1994), the wife's arm around her husband's back accentuates the closeness of the group. The artist's intention should be carried out all around a free-standing sculpture, without any angle appearing to be an afterthought.

Occasionally weavers, such as the tapestry artist Jon Eric Riis (American, b. 1945), have ventured into free-standing pieces. His three tapestries of five-foot tall African-American babies holding guns is unusual for his work, but it still has the detailed and meaningful content found in his coats that hang from the wall and open to expose complex imagery inside.

Meeting Three: Trial and Error in Three Dimensions

Figure 3.3. Jon Eric Riis, *Babes in Arms*, 2001. 66x28x8." Courtesy of the artist.

180 Degrees

"Relief" is the term used in sculpture to describe a work attached to a wall. The viewer usually sees it straight on, but can move from right to left to note how light and shadow affect the three-dimensional piece. Look at how effective Sheila Hick's Rainforest (Figure 3.4) is from the side.

While a relief is usually hung vertically on a wall, remember that a weaving that lies on the floor or a table will also be viewed from 180 degrees. Pile rugs, particularly ryas, play with light and shadows. As you sample and prototype your three-dimensional weaving, including those intended for the floor or table, ensure that they work from all possible viewing angles.

Figure 3.4. Sheila Hicks. *Rainforest*, about 1975. Silk, linen, and cotton. Renwick Gallery. Copyright Sheila Hicks, courtesy of Sikkema Jenkins& Co., New York. Photography by Art Poskanzer is licensed under cc by 2.0.

Suspended

A suspended piece will be seen from 360 degrees and possibly from above or below, thus it has additional issues that need to be considered. Beginning in the early 1930s, the Abstractionist Alexander Calder (American, 1898-1976) suspended basic geometric shapes that all moved independently, called kinetic mobiles. Today it isn't unusual to see a sculpture that moves with the air currents.

Innovative Weaving

Wearable art could also be considered a contemporary expression of 360-degree sculpture that hangs from the human body. Note the sculptural aspects of the outfit in Figure 3.5 by the Italian designer label Krizia. Search "wearable art" on the web, and you will be surprised by all the sculptural exploration of today's clothing designers.

Figure 3.5. Krizia, *Tuta a ventaglio*, 1981. Musei Mazzucchelli, Museum of Fashion and Costume, Ciliverghe of Mazzano, Italy.

Mass and Space

Figure 3.6. Tom Gingras, *Pegasus*, 1980. Steel, 25x21x15"

Mass is the term used to describe the solid parts of a sculpture that interact with the space it occupies. The sculptor can build the mass so that space can only be seen outside the piece, the mass can also be pierced with space, or the mass can open up to it. Another approach is to have the mass reach out into space. Until the 20th Century, a sculpture's mass was usually vertical and rather contained. *Pegasus* by Tom Gingras (American, b. 1949) demonstrates the exaggerated use of mass reaching out into and being pierced by space. The process of building a sculpture of welded steel allows the exuberant expression of mass and space not possible in marble and bronze.

You can look at a weaving's use of mass and space in much the same way as a sculptor. Consider the spaces within your fringing treatment. Does the openness of the fringe support or distract from the mass of the piece? Would an area of an open weave, such as leno, add interest? If you are designing a free-standing or other three-dimensional weaving, is there a way you can make it appear more dynamic by reaching further out into space?

Meeting Three: Trial and Error in Three Dimensions

Proportion

Well-defined rules of proportion for the human form, first developed by the Greek Polycleitus around 450 BCE, were usually followed carefully in Western sculpture until 1900. Adjustments were made when necessary, such as for a figure high up on a building's frieze that required a head to be larger in proportion to the normal human body in order to compensate for the distance and angle from which it was seen from the ground.

Ancient proportion guidelines, such as the Golden Ratio, are still helpful, but can be treated more loosely within today's sculpture, as long as your intention is communicated effectively. Do the proportions in your design, including color, texture, height, width, depth, etc., highlight what is most important for the piece? We will look more at proportion in Meeting 5: Building Art into Your Craft.

Detail

The amount of detail used to move the eye around and through a sculpture has changed as different styles evolved over time. One of the most significant developments in Modernism was Minimalism, where detail became an anathema. Minimalists reduced and abstracted forms to their most basic shapes, eliminating ornamentation or applied color. Any color was usually natural to the material. Geometric shapes were often arranged in a symmetrical order.

A Minimalist sculpture often had no supporting base, which had been a required element for thousands of years. Although there is color in *Cubeweave* by Jim Isermann (American, b. 1955), the way the basic cubes are organized and otherwise unadorned are typical of the style. Louise Nevelson (Ukrainian, 1899-1988) used plenty of detail in her found wood constructions, but balanced that complexity by painting everything one color, often black.

When you look at a sculpture, observe how much detail is there.

Do you usually like a lot of detail that supports the piece or are you drawn to a more minimalist style in your work?

Figure 3.7. Jim Isermann. *Cubeweave*, Installation view from Galleri Ynglingagatan 1, 1997. Hand-woven cloth, foam cubes. Courtesy of Artist.

Becoming aware of your own attraction to or dislike of detail in sculpture can help you shape your own style of weaving.

Textural Contrast

Variations in texture, such as smooth, shiny areas versus crosshatching, have always been a method of creating more interest in a sculptural piece. The wood Buddha in Figure 3.8 is rich with variety from the finely rubbed areas on the shoulder and knees to his curly hair.

Innovative Weaving

Needless to say, textural contrast will also enliven your weaving. Velvets, corduroys, and knotted piles are all age-old methods of creating texture in weaving. Contrasting areas with more or less dimension carry the eye across your piece.

Experimenting with texture has occupied many hand weavers in recent years. Organizations, such as Complex Weavers (www.complex-weavers.org), encourage innovation in three-dimensional structure and weaves, while the vendors at weaving conferences provide a seemingly endless variety of crepe, metal, and plastic yarns, in addition to beads and unusual materials that can add dimension to your weaving. Books and classes show you how to master overspun singles and collapsed weaves.

While all these techniques and materials are available to you, there is always room for your own innovative idea. How might you develop your own way to add texture to your weaving? Or is there a way to combine your weaving with something else of a much different texture to create a sculptural piece?

Figure 3.8. Balinese Buddha, wood.

WSSA member Linda Yeatts pulled together several of her unused projects with garden objects, like clay pots for the breasts, to create *Warrior Weaving Woman* (Figure 3.9). The wire supports became framing for a woven skirt. Textural variations provide much of the interest in this piece.

Figure 3.9. Linda Yeatts, *Warrior Weaving Woman*, 2015. Found garden objects, knitting, handweaving.

Contrast in Light and Shadow

The contrast between light and shadow is a common way to create interest and draw the viewer into a sculpture. Notice how Pablo Gargallo (Spanish, 1881-1934) shaped the eye sockets in Figure 3.10 to create sympathy for his characters. Gargallo's work became more

Figure 3.10. Pablo Gargallo, *The Humble.*, 1904. Cast bronze. National Art Museum of Catalonia, Barcelona, Spain.

Meeting Three: Trial and Error in Three Dimensions

abstract under the influence of Pablo Picasso, but his effective use of light and shadow remained. Light and shadow is what lets us see the physical texture in a weaving. Collapsed weaves, knotted piles, differential shrinkage, and the dynamic action of stainless steel yarns are all opportunities for you to create a sculptural play of light and shadow, without building an actual free-standing or relief sculpture.

Balance

Obviously, how the sculptor has stabilized his or her work to prevent it from falling over has always been an important consideration. A traditional figurative sculpture's ability to stand on its own depended upon the proper balance of the heavy marble or bronze material. The Greek concept of "contraposto" was about balancing the figure around a central post.

Stronger materials and techniques in the 20th Century, such as welded steel, provided the ability to stretch out into space and thus challenge the long-held rules of balance, using compositional imbalance to create a dynamic sense of movement. Tom Gingras says that he finds inspiration in the balanced flexibility and strength of the DNA double helix, that is similar to the elongated S-curves of the Egyptian, Greco-Roman, and late Renaissance sculptors. Keeping that image in mind is particularly important the more open and dynamic the piece. (See Figure 3.6.)

Notice, as you look at a sculpture, does it look stable or does it appear in motion due to its compositional instability? How might you build physical stability into your free-standing work, while also creating a sense of dynamic movement? Stability can also be a challenge in wearable art. How do you ensure your scarf or garment maintains the three-dimensional effect you imagine, rather than falling flat?

Support

Defying the force of gravity has always been a major challenge for sculptors. Marble stands firmly as long as there is plenty of support underneath it. Outstretched marble arms, often carved separately and attached to the body, were vulnerable to breaking loose from their support over time, because of their heavy weight. Some sculpture, such as that made of bronze, starts out with an internal wire framework called an armature to support the clay that will be carved to create a cast. A central armature of some type could also be used to vertically support other materials, including hand woven fabric. Creating a free-standing sculpture is more of a challenge for those of us committed to loom weaving, unless of course you weave with wire. We more normally strive to produce soft cloth with a nice drape. Even a coarser tapestry will puddle to the floor without support.

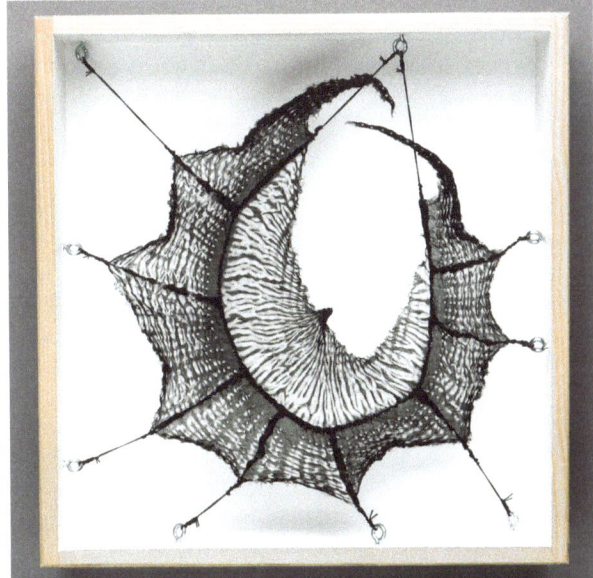

Figure 3.11. Mo Kelman, *Rota*, 2011. Shibori dyed and shaped silk, wooden box, 9x9x3" Courtesy of the artist.

While a sculptural relief may be somewhat easier to support than a free-standing piece, a relief will still present some technical challenges. Obviously consideration of the weight is important, but the maker needs to also determine if the support will be hidden or integrated into the piece. The attachments to the wall shouldn't be an unintended distraction.

Mo Kelman (American, b. 1952) considers the support issues early in her design process and believes that the exposure of all the attachments, including meticulously executed knots, careful wrapping, and eye screws, allows her work to project an honesty and openness.

A piece that hangs from the ceiling comes with its own problems. Certainly considerations of its weight and the most acceptable support for the space where it will hang are important issues. A gallery or other facility might not allow holes in the ceiling or the ceiling may be too high to safely reach. Also the hardware shouldn't distract from the design of the piece, but should appear as an intentional part of it. While you don't want to get distracted by these details during brainstorming, do spend time early in your design process to work through the support issues, at least enough to know if the project is at all feasible.

Content

While all sculpture was figural before the 20th Century, Minimalists removed all such content from their work. "It is what it is," as is said today when nothing needs to be read into it. Other Modernist sculptors have important ideas they wanted to communicate, such as concerns about war, the environment, violence, but certainly heroic figures and heroism became less the subject of sculptors after the 1950s. Look again at Jon Eric Riis's *Babes in Arms* in Figure 3.3. The relatively large 5-foot scale amplifies his statement about guns in the hands of mere children.

As you brainstorm in the exercises at the study group meeting, think about a message you would like to communicate with your piece or will you go the Minimalist route and have it be just be about the piece and its originality?

Risk Experimenting with Completely New Ideas

The more you allow yourself to generate original ideas, the more you will find yourself exploring techniques that are outside your current skill set. And the more innovative the ideas are, the less chance that you are going to find easy instructions on how to carry them out. If you aren't willing to step into the unknown, your creative idea will likely not see the light of day.

Persistent prototyping and retries are required for any innovative idea to reach reality. Ernest Hemingway is said to have rewritten the ending of *Farewell to Arms* sixty-seven times. The determined physical efforts and inventiveness of the master weaver Peter Collingwood (British, 1922-2008) might be even more impressive. Throughout his career as a weaver, he pushed the craft, developed new techniques, adapted his loom to effectively work with the new techniques, and created tools to more quickly dress the loom and ensure the highest quality of his final product.

Collingwood kept a diary from 1996 through 1997 documenting the process of creating one of his large sculptural microgauze pieces for the Cultural Centre in Kiryu, Japan. The piece would be nine strips each 32 inches wide and 16 feet long, using a newly developed stainless steel yarn the size of 2-ply carpet wool. Collingwood repeatedly stopped the tedious and physically challenging weaving process to develop yet another way to keep the heavy, slippery yarn moving through the loom squarely.

Meeting Three: Trial and Error in Three Dimensions

In the three months of work, there are at least fifty-four points where he met a problem that required him to stop to modify his loom, such as replacing the breast beam and knee bar with rollers or develop jerry-rigged tools that helped with such tasks as threading the rigid heddles with the springy yarn. Needless to say, shipping 198 lbs of the packed piece to Japan and hanging it to its best advantage at the Cultural Centre presented even more challenges. Collingwood admits in his diary to cursing at points of greatest frustrations and thinking through problems in the middle of the night as he attempted to fall asleep.

It is easy to say that Peter Collingwood was a genius, with intellectual and creative gifts much greater than you or I. On the other hand, current thinking questions the idea that genius plays a major role in creativity. Collingwood's greatest strength might have been his willingness to work through problem after problem, accepting the challenges, and enjoying finding the successful solution. Like most innovations, each solution would often result in yet another unseen problem he would have to solve. But he would keep going. That persistence is what it takes to create something new.

In order to bring that original idea into reality, you have to be able to push past the desire to quit and to avoid simply going back to the familiar. Each time there is another failure, learn from it, and use your Open Creativity to determine how to overcome it. Collingwood sampled his Kiryu piece in linen, did numerous calculations and color drawings, and even tested hanging it before it was sent to Japan. That careful planning didn't prevent all problems, but certainly cuts down on them.

The sculptor Lee Bontecou (American, b. 1931) is another example of a persistent innovator. She has been experimenting and producing unusual sculpture since the late 1950s. All of her sculpture was produced with her own hands. She was not like most marble and bronze sculptors who modeled in clay and then handed the completion over to skilled artisans.

Over fifty years, Bontecou developed sculpture that involved engineering challenges and learning new skills, while also having a consistency of purpose and theme. Her many detailed graphite drawings of gas masks and eyes show her exploring ideas that she then incorporated into her three-dimensional work. Her series of over 6-foot steel and canvas reliefs increased in complexity over the eight years she made them, as if each one was a prototype for the piece that followed. Engineering issues required significant planning and testing, such as how to hang a piece bigger and heaver than her on a gallery wall, how to make the large piercings in these reliefs as dark as possible when they are really only 18 inches deep, and how to attach canvas to the steel frame in a meaningful, yet effective way.

Bontecou's joy in her experimentation seems to be far more important to her than any commercial success. While she left New York City in the early 1970's for a Pennsylvania farm to raise her daughter, she continued to explore new materials, skills, and techniques, but she didn't exhibit her work for over twenty years. From her perspective, the pressure of gallery shows prevented her from experimenting and creating innovative work that meant something to her.

Once on the farm, Bontecou left the welded steel and canvas work behind and began to produce oversized flowers and fishes made in vacuum-formed transparent plastic, and then began making free-standing and hanging bird skulls and insects with welded steel, white porcelain, wire, and cloth. Only by persisting through repeated attempts and a willingness to step into unknown skills and engineering challenges could such work be produced.

While all of us may not likely achieve the consistent innovation of a Lee Bontecou or Peter Collingwood, we can be inspired by their willingness to challenge themselves and persist through frustrating failed attempts. They were innovators only because they spent time prototyping and learning from their mistakes.

Detailed designs and sampling your weaving can feel like you are being kept from actually making that fantastic piece you envision. However, acceptance of the focused process of prototyping brings you closer to that dream, particularly if you are trying to make something that is uniquely yours. When you rush through, or skip, the detailed design process and sampling, you may be left with a sense of failure when the project goes terribly wrong. Worse case you may give up on an idea that has wonderful potential.

WSSA member Bob Bateman's suspended triple weave, *Enigma*, started out as simply an exercise from Else Regensteiner's *Weaver's Study Course*. He had created a long warp to make samples, along with experimenting with ideas in Jennifer Moore's *Doubleweave* book. Serendipitously he had purchased a spool of ball chain on deep discount from his favorite hardware store that was going out of business. The spool sat on a shelf with his yarn, when ideas converged and he saw how the sett was perfect to work in the ball chain as weft. Bateman's relaxed sampling surely created an atmosphere for this innovative weaving to emerge.

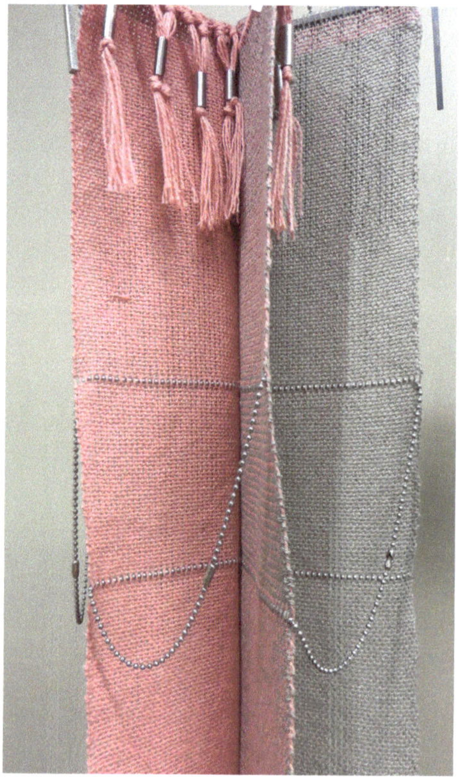

Exercises

Exercise 3.1 (30 minutes)

Ten Minutes   Study any one of the Figures in this chapter. Consider how you might incorporate depth, shadow, and light into a handwoven piece that would hang on the wall or stand on its own. Sketch or write down as many ideas as you can in your notebook.

Twenty Minutes One at a time, share two or three of your ideas with the group and note any subsequent ideas that come to mind.

Exercise 3.2 (30 minutes)

Figure 3.12. Bob Bateman, *Enigma*, 2014-2015. Triple weave, cotton, metal.

Ten Minutes   Continue to develop your ideas in Exercise 3.1. How might you pierce your work to create voids or space? How could you add a sense of permanence or preciousness? Is there a message you would like to communicate? Sketch or write as many ideas as you can in your notebook.

Twenty Minutes One at a time, share two or three of your ideas with the group and note any subsequent ideas that come to mind.

Conclusion

Sculpture in the 20th and 21st Century can provide exciting inspiration for the weaver. Abstraction, Minimalism, and a bunch of other isms present lots of different ideas for how you can play with three dimensions in your loom weaving, whether it is for a functional piece, such as a rug, wearable art, or a free-standing, relief, or ceiling-hung piece.

Meeting Three: Trial and Error in Three Dimensions

On the other hand, most likely experimentation in any of these arenas is going to cause you to run into engineering challenges that will require your patient experimentation. If you find yourself ready to give up the effort, remember that continuing to solve each problem you come upon will not only bring you satisfaction, but by sharing your effort in the study group you might help others overcome limitations they may also be experiencing.

Further Resources for Inspiration

Collins, Judith. *Sculpture Today*. New York: Phaidon Press Inc., 2007.

Dalgaard, Lotte. *Magical Materials to Weave*. North Pomfret, Vermont: Trafalgar Square Books, 2011.

Eckert, Carol. Contemporary Basketry, http://contemporarybasketry.blogspot.com

Fabrics That Go Bump, ed. Madelyn van der Hoogt. Sioux Falls, SD: XRX, Inc., 2002.

Field, Anne. *Collapse Weave; Creating Three-Dimensional Cloth*. London: A&C Black Publishers, 2008.

Google Images: "Wearable Art"

Sculpture magazine

MEETING FOUR: ALIVE WITH THE SOUND OF MUSIC

Weaving sounds together in different patterns creates music. This chapter looks at the manipulation of those aural patterns and how you might apply them visually to your weaving. The development of music, like that of weaving, depended upon both Open and Focused Creativity. The most Open musicians have pushed the art form in new directions, while also appropriating from what has come before. The most Focused have created reproducible structures in the form of aural tradition, sheet music, and now YouTube, ensuring that musical innovations can be incorporated into new work and passed down to future generations.

This chapter explores some of the issues that music and weaving share, including the legal and ethical questions around borrowing ideas from other artists. A "rehearsal" piece encourages you to use movement and rhythm to bring symmetry and balance into your time at the loom. One exercise explores creativity through the music and lyrics of Stephen Sondheim. Another encourages you to develop your own interpretation of an Anni Albers weaving..

A Very Brief History of Music

Response to music is in our genes, which can be seen even in Macaque monkeys who drum rhythmically on their chests to show social dominance. Sounds a lot like a heavy metal band, doesn't it? We only need our hands, feet, or voice to make music. As long as there is a repeated rhythm of sounds and silences, we experience music. A single melody of different notes over time enriches the sound, even if it is only drums tuned to different pitches.

The development of music from its earliest human form to the present is all about the balance between Open and Focused Creativity. Musicians must dedicate hundreds, if not thousands, of practice hours in order to play their instruments properly and to coordinate their sounds with other performers. In addition, all music has an established structure that both the performers and the audience know well, even if it might be subconscious. To deviate too much from that structure creates what may be experienced by the listeners as simply noise.

On the other hand, the incredible variety of music available around the world is only possible because innovators push those established forms into new sounds. The innovations are rarely as earth shattering as they may seem at the time, such as when Bob Dylan played familiar folk structures on an electric guitar at a Newport Folk Festival in 1965. Whether it is the increased complexity of Mozart's work, the experimental instruments of Sun Ra, the jazz improvisations of Sonny Rollins, or the smoothness of Jay Z's rap cadence, their innovations still has enough familiarity for audiences to understand and thus appreciate.

Figure 4.1 Sonny Rollins, Monterey Jazz Festival, 2011

Innovative Weaving

Music plays an important, if not central, role, in most people's lives. Of all the arts, music is considered the language of feeling, even as intense as ecstasy as can be seen in a Sufi dance or a Grateful Dead concert. In addition to tapping into our deepest emotions, music has always been used to coordinate human movement, such as laying railroad track, walking the bride and her attendants down the aisle, or Scottish women around a table finishing a woven blanket.

Norman Kennedy, winner of a 2003 NEA National Heritage Fellowship, travels around to weaving guilds, teaching them the traditional Scottish waulking songs that were used to maintain the steady rhythm of women whacking and moving damp wool yardage around a table to full or shrink it into a dense, warm blanket. While mechanization eliminated much of the need for such work songs, we humans will always use music to bring us together through synchronized movements and to share of our deepest emotions.

Applying Musical Elements to Weaving

Music theory is rich in methods for creating variety, while also maintaining a recognizable form. The Broadway musical composer and lyricist Stephen Sondheim (American, b. 1930) said:

> There is something about the conscious use of form in any art that says to the customer, "This is worth saying." Without form the idea, the intention and, most important, the effect, no matter how small in ambition becomes flaccid...."

Sondheim has been more than generous with his insights into music and creativity, with two books (*Finishing the Hat* and *Look! I've Made a Hat*) that break down his lyric writing process into detail, song by song, and a book of interviews, written by Mark Horowitz (*Sondheim on Music*) that analyses Sondheim's scores now stored in the Library of Congress. His thoughts about the use of different elements in music can provide limitless inspiration for your weaving. An understanding of how the following elements weave together to produce a piece of music can help you analyze your own and others work and thus enrich your own designs.

Tone

Tone is the highness or lowness of a sound or note relative to any other note, as illustrated below in the two measures from Sondheim's song "Putting It Together." Low tones vibrate more slowly, higher tones more quickly.

The key is a selected note or set of notes (chord) that provides a sense of rest. The melody will move around that key, thus create a tension, and then come to rest back at the key note, creating a resolution.

When writing the musical *Sunday in the Park with George*, inspired by Georges Seurat's painting *A Sunday on La Grande Jatte*, Sondheim considered assigning a note to each of twelve colors on George's palette, so that when George sings the word "blue," he would use a specific note. He quickly realized that this approach was too restrictive for him to create an effective melody and gave up the idea.

Meeting Four: Alive with the Sound of Weaving

However, we, as weavers, can assign notes to colors of warp ends, as Tracy Kaestner described in the September/October 2000 issue of *Handwoven*, which was dedicated to musical inspirations. She used a small section of Johann Sebastian Bach's Minuet 3 to create stripes in nine different colors in a goose-eye twill.

The same issue of *Handwoven* shows yet another method for designing from sheet music. Phyllis Hirsch assigned a shaft to each note in a jazz piece written by her husband, to create a weaving pattern. She then tweaked the design somewhat to avoid long floats and create symmetry.

Figure 4.2 Tracy Kaestner. *Minuet 3 by Johann Sebastian* Bach. From Handwoven, September/October 2000. Photograph by Joe Coca. Courtesy of Interweave. Copyright 2000 by Interweave.

Developing a weaving design inspired by the specific notes from a piece of music that has a special significance to you can be a satisfying way to make your work original and personal. Take advantage of the website SheetMusic-Direct.us, which provides thousands of scores available to download for less than five dollars each.

Melody

A set of single notes or tones that move up and down on a scale with a rhythmic spacing is considered a melody. Sondheim developed a two-note melody or motif, usually sung as "I wish," that wove through the whole score of the Broadway musical *Into the Woods*. The show's theme centered around wishing for something one doesn't have, thus all the main characters had their own song that used that small motif in the melody and the lyrics.

A short melodic motif might provide the right number of notes to use as a repeat in a weaving design. You could assign specific colors or texture of yarns in a specific order according to the notes in a motif. Then create solid stripes, but insert the motif in regular or irregular spacing across the warp.

You can also create an inversion of the motif, by using the same colors or textures, but reversing the order. The eye will still see the relationship, as the ear does in a musical inversion, but you have created variety.

You might find it fun to play your favorite song on iTunes or YouTube and listen for the parts of the piece that particularly touch you. Then experiment with different approaches to transforming that melody into a repeat for a weaving design. It's perfectly acceptable to make adjustments to the design to avoid floats or simply to make the design more attractive to your own aesthetic.

Tempo

The speed that the notes are played is called the tempo. The repetition of woven stripes in the warp might be seen as representing a tempo, with variations in the repetition showing a change in speed.

Innovative Weaving

Narrow stripes evolving into wider stripes and back into narrow stripes would be a good way to represent a variation in fast and slow tempos.

Tracey Kaestner was using tempo when she used a different number of warp ends to represent how long each note (color) was held. Each note was assigned 11 ends, except for a dotted half note, where she assigned 33 ends, and a note played twice in succession, which she assigned 22 ends. See Figure 4.2.

Rhythm

A strong sound (called a beat) repeated in a regular pattern with spaces in between is called a rhythm. The tempo will define how fast or slow the rhythm is played. A steady rhythm allows us to predict what is to come and helps synchronize the movements of the musicians and expectations of the audience. Whether it is two-stepping with a partner around the dance floor to a country song, pogoing in a mosh pit, moving in a kickboxing class as the instructor yells "Tempo!" and "Half time!", or being calmed by serene music in the dentist's chair, we are responding to the rhythm, exactly like our forebears hundreds of thousands of years ago.

However, we need a variety in that steady rhythm. Small flourishes here and there keep the sound from becoming boring. Short changes in the drum pattern often happen in rock and country music to signal a change from one section of a song to the next, while also providing variety.

Of course, these ideas can also be applied to weaving. Control of the rhythmic repetition of pattern, colors, and textures allow the viewer to predict what they see next as their eyes move across the piece. Intended changes in that rhythm create a welcomed surprise. Borders are a common way to start and stop the steady beat of a pattern that might otherwise seem boring. This goes back to what Sondheim said about people wanting to see structure and form, but they just don't want to be bored by it.

Volume/Dynamics

The loudness or quietness of a sound or note is the volume. Like all the other musical elements, controlled variety helps accentuate what is important and directs our focus. Those variations in volume are called the dynamics of the piece. Even the loudest rock bands play with dynamics for effect. The variations in volume of the individual voices and instruments during a piece contribute to the work's texture.

Figure 4.3 Whiskey Shivers, Antone's, Austin, TX, 2011.

We also use the terms "loud" and "quiet" when we talk about colors and visual textures. Loud is overly flashy, with patterns and colors that seem to clash with each other. Quiet is often greyed, almost seeming to disappear, not bright or showy. Thus we can play with dynamics in our weaving. Would an occasional change in "volume" provide a needed spark? Intentional variation in the dynamics of the piece shows that you have control of your design, and the piece ultimately becomes more satisfying to the viewer.

Meeting Four: Alive with the Sound of Weaving

Timbre

The quality of sound that distinguishes it from another sound of the same pitch and volume is the timbre. The saxophone and the vocalist may be singing the same note at the same volume, but they obviously sounds different. Bernadette Peters (American, b. 1948) played both George's love interest in *Sunday in the Park with George* and the witch in *Into the Woods* on Broadway. The timbre of her voice is unique, described as vulnerable, girly, rounded, and with lots of vibrato (soft variations in amplitude), which creates the perfect emotion for her parts. Christina Aguilera has her own unique timbre to her voice, unless she is impersonating the individual qualities in another singer, such as Cher. The timbre in voices is often called light, airy, grainy, powerful, strong, thick, or raspy.

Possibly we can consider each type of yarn and color as having its own timbre. A strand of red linen is much different than one of red silk in the same size. The intensity of color, the sheen, the weight, and the feel are all different, yet each is beautiful in its uniqueness. We can create surprise and interest in our designs by combining different yarns and playing with their different qualities (or timbre). Suddenly the cloth becomes more visually interesting, even in plain weave, when we work in different textures of yarn, no matter how subtle, as long as we are not affecting the integrity of the piece. However your choices still need to reflect your control of the materials by picking yarns appropriate for their intended use and washability.

Another analogy of timbre might be your own personal touch that you bring to your work, no matter how much you might try to suppress it. Judith Powell Krone was inspired by the September/October 2000 *Handwoven* issue on music, but added her own touch by including the composer and the piece's title into the design with name drafting, thus assigning letters to shafts.

Figure 4.4 Judith Powell Krone, *Shubert's Serenade*. Shawl, extended point twill, cotton, wool, silk. Handwoven, March/April 2003. Photography by Joe Coca. Courtesy of Interweave. Copyright 2003 by Interweave.

Franz Schubert's *Serenade* had strong childhood memories for her, so she used a motif of notes and their durations from the piece for the four colors and their stripe width and then the phrase "Franz Peter Shubert Serenade" to develop the pattern. She assigned each letter to a shaft (AIQY=1, BJRZ=2, CKS=3, DLT=4, EMU=5, FNV=6, GOW=7, HPX=8) and then added warp ends where necessary to create a point twill.

Krone's piece looks significantly different than all the weavings in the 2000 issue of *Handwoven* that inspired her. You also would benefit from embracing your uniqueness, your own combination of aesthetics, skills, color preferences, etc., to create your "timbre." Of course, all of that will naturally evolve as you gain experience as a weaver. A saxophone doesn't need to sound like a ukulele. Be true to your own voice.

Harmony

Two or more notes played or sung at the same time that produce a pleasing sound is called harmony. If the sound isn't pleasing, it is considered dissonance. Harmony can also be said to be the vertical aspect of music, rather than the horizontal movement of the melody. In Western music,

Innovative Weaving

a harmonic chord is made up of one note as the bass or lowest in tone followed by two or more higher notes played at the same time, with the note between each of them not played. For instance, a C chord is comprised of C, E, and G. When notes next to each other on the scale are played at the same time, we call it dissonance and it sounds almost like a mistake.

Like chords in music, harmony of two or more colors can be created in our weaving. In her book *Color Works*, Deb Menz uses harmony to describe various combinations of hues around the color wheel, such as split complementary harmony, double split complementary harmony, triad harmony, and double triad harmony. She also defines several other "chords" that are comprised of four and six different colors that work well together.

Just like in music, you can choose to create a piece that is not harmonious, that is jarring to the eye. But if you want to design your version of a punk band, make sure the viewer understands that this is your intention, rather than that you just didn't know what you were doing. By thoughtfully selecting where to apply the disharmony while showing you understand the underlying form, you show you are still in control, no matter how out of control your piece may appear at first viewing.

Tension and Resolution

Tension is created in music by playing with the listener's expectations, thus holding off what obviously should happen next. Harmonic dissonance is often used to create tension. If and when a musical piece eventually returns to that expectation, it is said to have reached resolution. Listeners may not even be aware of what they are waiting for, since it is so engrained in the style and traditions of any particular culture's music. Tension can be built around the melody, rhythm, or harmony going in unexpected directions. Daryl Hall and John Oats "She's Gone" from their *Abandoned Luncheonette* album is an example of the power of dissonance, seeming to use all three forms of tension, building to a crescendo towards the end, followed by its resolution.

Stephen Sondheim talks about intentionally using a dissonant phrase to play against the suggestion of a bugle in Act I Scene 1 of *Passion*. A three-note bugle phrase is followed by a lower dissonant accompaniment. Sondheim repeats this small phrase often throughout the play to create tension.

Attempting to understand all the mechanics and potential of dissonance without a music theory education is as mindboggling as attempting to understand the mechanics of quad weave without a thorough understanding of weaving technical terms. But just like in music, we know when we see a dissonance in a weaving, when combined colors aren't in harmony, when the rhythm of motifs or stripes seems odd, and when the melody of texture, colors, pattern, and execution just don't seem right. The trick for the creative weaver is to be able incorporate tension somewhere in our weaving, but to be in enough control to know when and how to resolve it.

Paying attention to how you are going to resolve tension is particularly important when you are using asymmetry in a design. Are you choosing to make the piece feel balanced and thus resolved, despite being asymmetrical, or are you wanting to make the piece feel off balance? As always, do what is needed to make 'em think you meant to do that.

Improvisation

A musician is said to improvise when he/she "composes and performs without previous preparation." Clearly that definition can't be taken literally. Successful jazz musicians and rap artists have committed many years of preparation in order to perform their music "on the fly." Working within a well-rehearsed format, particularly if they are performing with other musicians, allows the improvisation to surprise and thrill the audience while allowing everyone to appreciate

Meeting Four: Alive with the Sound of Weaving

the musicians' skill and control amongst the seeming chaos. The jazz saxophonist John Coltrane (American, 1926-1967) improvised with the melody and harmony. The pianist Franz Liszt (Hungarian, 1811-1886) was said to have great precision, including an absolute tempo, but he would improvise harmonies, add in trills, and play with the rhythm to add emotion and build tension.

An appearance of improvisation can also be exciting when we see it in a woven piece. However we want to know that the maker is in control. Too much chaos begins to look like the thrift store rag rug with wavering selvedges and uneven beat. Saori weaving is most effective when we can see that the maker has not let the materials get the best of her. Her final choices of colors and textures might have been made at the last minute, but they were conscious choices, thoughtfully made.

Genre

Pieces of music that conform to a distinguishable form or subject matter is said to be part of a particular a genre, such as reggae, country, classical, world, or electronica. When someone buys a cd or goes to a concert she/he is expecting music that fits their expectations of that genre. Musicians that attempt to make a living from their art usually find that in order to sign a recording contract or get radio play they must shape their music to meet those expectations.

Musicians that rebel against those limitations, such as Austin singer-songwriter Bob Schneider, find alternative methods of getting their music out, such as using Kickstarter to finance an album, rather than signing a record contract, and selling cds, shirts, and bobbleheads at smaller venues, rather than the big arenas. The financial rewards are significantly smaller for a performer like Schneider, but he enjoys being able to write in whatever genre inspires him at the time, be it hip hop, jazz, alternate country, or romantic Christmas songs.

Figure 4.5 Bob Schneider at The Roost, Austin, TX, 2015.

If you want financial success as a weaver, the market, though obviously smaller than that of music, has much the same limitations. Our "genres" include traditional, wearable art, tapestry, Saori, Scandinavian, home décor, and others. Customers expect to see your range of work with a specific genre, within its specific rules of form. However, just like a musician, how do you stand out within that genre? What makes you different and innovative?

You can emulate Bob Schneider and enjoy experimenting with different styles, learning as you go and enjoying the process. At some point, you may find one genre you want to focus on, but meanwhile "Follow your bliss."

Innovate a Little, Borrow a Lot

Sondheim's book *Finishing the Hat* provides much insight into creativity, inspiration, and artistic borrowing. Most of the composer's work was inspired by someone else's artistic endeavor. But his

Innovative Weaving

transformation of the original work into his own expression is a model for all of us on how to stay on the right side of the copyright law.

Take a look at the "trail of inspiration" below to see how the song "Putting It Together" came to be and what it subsequently lead to. Note how each of Sondheim's collaborators brought new perspectives and ideas to the table. Figure 4.6 shows *A Sunday on La Grande Jatte*.

Inspiration	Art Piece	Artist
Photograph at a birthday party	*Photograph* (play) 1920	Gertrude Stein, playwright
Photograph by Gertrude Stein	*Photograph* (play adaptation) 1977. Used poster of George Seurat's *A Sunday on La Grande Jatte* (1884) in the set	James Lapine, director and adaptor
Poster of *A Sunday on La Grande Jatte* (painting) at the play *Photograph*.	*Sunday in the Park with George* (musical play) 1984	Stephen Sondheim, music and lyrics; James Lapine, book
"Putting It Together" (song from *Sunday in the Park with George*)	"Putting It Together" (song with revised lyrics), 1985	Barbra Streisand, vocalist; Stephen Sondheim, music and lyrics
"Putting It Together" (song from *Sunday in the Park with George*) and other Sondheim songs	*Putting It Together* (musical review) 1992	Stephen Sondheim, music and lyrics; Stephen Sondheim and Julia McKenzie, book

Sondheim easily admits to borrowing chords and other musical ideas from other musicians, and even says he gets much of his ideas from the early 20th Century French composer Maurice Ravel. The point isn't that Sondheim is unique in his admitted borrowing, it is that he is just like every other creative person, working within a set of standards, learning from the masters in the craft, and striving to reassemble the known in new and surprising ways. In his interviews for the Library of Congress, Sondheim often describes himself as "stealing" ideas from other musicians. He regularly listens to music from around the world, looking for bits that excite him. But he says he doesn't consciously think about borrowing an idea, "it just lodges somewhere back here and it will probably show up."

Sondheim is known for effectively and creatively using pastiche in some of his plays, such as *Assassins*, where each number reflects the music of the time period when an attempt was made on an US president's life, from Lincoln to Reagan. He says it is quite easy for

Figure 4.6 Georges Seurat, *A Sunday on La Grande Jatte*, 1884. Oil on canvas, 81 ¾ x 121 ¼ in. Helen Birch Bartlett Memorial Collection, The Art Institute of Chicago.

him to copy the styles of those time periods because "it's just in my bones. I know the literature, because I love it." But he doesn't use all the other musicians' ideas, only enough that the audience can recognize the style, the rest is his invention.

Computerization has allowed a musician to not only borrow someone else's musical ideas, but also to use the actual sound of someone else's playing in their own work. One of the earliest example of sampling occurred when a six-second drum break in a 1969 recording of "Amen Brothers" by the Winstons was cut out, looped upon itself, and used for the rhythm tract at a dance party. Those six seconds became the steady rhythm behind many hip hop and electronic music recordings from the 1990s on. More sophisticated technology allowed the samples to be broken down into individual beats and rearranged. At this point, the Amen break loops and other rhythm samples are ubiquitous, even showing up in television commercials.

As weavers, we also are building on the innovators before us. Fifty years ago, the master weaver Harriet Tidball wrote about originality in her *Weaver's Book*, as paraphrased below:

- Find patterns that are less used and interpret them in a new way.
- Avoid starting with a complex pattern. A simpler pattern-block allows for variation, interpretation, and innovation.
- Don't bother trying to be original. There is little possibility that you will come up with something that hasn't been done before. But you can bring a "fresh interpretation and a new idea to something already known."
- Forcing yourself to come up with something completely original "will betray itself in poor designing and inadequate function."

Sondheim and Tidball are telling you the same thing. Stand on the shoulders of those that came before you, but bring yourself to the table. (Mixed metaphor acknowledged).

Copyright Protection

When you stand on the shoulders of those that came before you, be careful not to tell an interviewer in a major publication that you took a record you liked and wrote something like it in a half hour, as Robin Thicke bragged about the creation of his and Pharrell William's song "Blurred Lines." Within the high profit world of the music industry, the originator of the inspiration or his family could easily take you to court and win. The differences amongst copyright infringement, accidental subliminal infringement (think of the musical ideas "lodged" in Sondheim's brain), and lawful borrowing will likely be argued in the courts for many more years, including issues around sampling. However musicians can now buy the rights to use many samples, including the Amen break, on the internet. However the originators, such as the Winstons, often do not see any of those profits.

As weavers, you will benefit from paying attention to the cases such as that of "Blurred Lines" in order to understand how the copyright laws might affect your own work, both as you are inspired by other weavers work and as you attempt to receive compensations for your creative work.

All art involves borrowing ideas from someone else. But we certainly don't want to stop creating out of fear of being accused of piracy. *Weaving Today* has a good guideline for weavers, entitled "Know Your Rights: Copyright 101 for Weavers." Essentially it says that you can make a scarf from a pattern in *Handwoven* exactly as written for yourself or as a gift, but you can't sell it without permission from the designer and *Handwoven*. You must significantly change the design in order to claim it as your own. Of course, "significantly" is ambiguous and why cases go to court.

Innovative Weaving

As weavers, the chances of multi-million dollar settlements are slimmer than slim. On the other hand, we all want to be ethical and maintain a good reputation in our small community of weavers. Suppose one day you were feeling out of ideas and wanted something to weave and chose a piece by Anni Albers (German, 1899-1932) as inspiration for your own work.

You could try to copy the work exactly. This would exercise your Focused Creativity skills. How do you reproduce the exact colors? You could even try to count the number of warps to get it just right. Little chance yours will look exactly like Albers, but you will learn something and hopefully break out of your creative block with a desire to design something of your own. On the other hand, because of the copyright laws you should not show this piece in public without getting permission from the Josef and Anni Albers Foundation and giving proper credit.

Another alternative is to use your Open Creativity to take off on the Albers piece by changing the spacing and colors. Or use the colors, but not the patterning. Possibly flip the warp and weft. If your design is different, but it still has a strong relationship to Albers' piece, you might want to add "homage to Anni Albers" or "after Anni Albers" to any description of your piece to give her proper credit.

It would be fun to have an exhibit of your study group's weaving all based on the same Albers' piece or that of another important weaver. However, remember that if you use an image in any publicity for the show, you need to get permission from the artist or their representatives.

Copyright law may seem like a pain in the neck, but on the other hand, it is intended to protect YOUR income and rights to your efforts as a creative person. Respect the creativity of other artists and you should be fine.

Rehearsal at the Loom

"Practice, practice, practice" is the mantra of every music teacher. Certainly that also applies to any of the fiber arts. The efficiency of dressing the loom, the evenness of your beat, and the straightness of your selvedges all depend upon the number of hours you consciously put at your "instrument." Your every movement and your concentration all contribute to the quality of your work. And just like a musician, the more hours you put into practicing to perfect all the movements, the more control you will have of the final result.

Music can also provide the background for your time at the loom, particularly when you choose the genre that most closely fits the rhythm of your shuttle tosses, beat, and treadling. The precision of the musician and dancer might be a model for our weaving. Harriet Tidball in *The Weaver's Book* published in 1961 compared music to weaving:

> Weaving itself is a rhythm, a rhythm which can carry much of the expressive feeling of dancing. For many, the highest pleasure can be attained from weaving only when the various movements of treadling, beating, shuttle-throwing and shuttle-catching are so coordinated that they flow as if to music. Each of these movements plays an important part in the full weaving cycle.

Jette Vandermeiden's *Weaving Basics: Ergonomics of Weaving* on YouTube provides a good approach to bringing rhythm and ergonomics to your weaving. Expanding on her ideas, the following steps provide a rehearsal of movement before you actually begin to weave. Each step allows you to practice the movements (the dance) of weaving, while also helping you observe your

Meeting Four: Alive with the Sound of Weaving

body to ensure you are balanced and adequately centered on your bench. You might add a little extra to your warp to run through this, but most steps are performed without actually weaving.

Step	Description	Observations
1	Put on some music with a comfortable slow beat.	
2	• Position your bench so that your feet can comfortably press the pedals. Center your body, shoulders relaxed and back. • Sit on the front part of the bench so your legs are able to freely move from the hips. • Bend your arms at the elbows and rest them on the breast beam.	Is your waist at the same height as the breast beam? Can your bend arms rest on the breast beam without raising your shoulders? If not, make the necessary adjustments to your bench.
3	• Imagine you have a shuttle in your right hand. • Rotate your lower arm out to the side as you would if you were throwing the shuttle and bring it back to the right selvedge. • Repeat 10 times with your right arm. • Repeat with your left arm.	Notice how that feels. Is there a difference between the rotation in the right and left arm? Attempt to make your movement symmetrical.
4	• Place an empty or unattached shuttle in the center of the warp. • Hold it in your right hand and rotate your arm out to the side in the same movement you used Step 3. • Bring it to the center of the warp and transfer the shuttle to left hand. • Transfer the shuttle back and forth from the hand to hand 10 times, keeping the movement symmetrical and rhythmic.	Are your spine still centered and your shoulders relaxed, but back?
5	• Create a shed. • Throw the shuttle back and forth with the same symmetrical movement. • Maintain the same range of motion with each arm. • Repeat 10 times.	Notice if one arm is better at this than the other.
6	• Pantomime grasping the beater in the center with your right hand and pulling it toward you. • Leave your left hand on the breast beam. • Lean back. Push the imaginary beater back, while moving forward. • Open your right hand and bring it to the breast beam.	Notice the feel of those muscles and the angle of your wrist and arm. Aim for a point at the exact center of the beater, but at a point in front where your arm is bent at a comfortable angle.

Innovative Weaving

Step	Description	Observations
	• Repeat 10 times. • Repeat the actions 10 times with your left hand, leaving your right hand on the breast beam.	
7	• Now actually pull the beater toward you with your right hand and lean back. • Alternate with your left hand. Repeat 10 times.	Watch where you place your hand. Practice getting your hand right in the center as you pull it towards you. Pay attention to the strength you are using to beat. Does it seem the same in both arms?
8	• Step on the tied-up treadle most to the right with your right foot. • Step on the tied-up treadle most to your left the left with your left foot. • Repeat 10 times.	Do you feel balanced in your movement? Is there another tie-up that would be more balanced and thus more efficient? Would a sliding bench be better, particularly if you often work with wide warps.
9	• Treadle to create a shed with your right foot. • Throw the empty shuttle with your right hand. • Beat with your right hand • Treadle with the opposite foot. • Push the beater back • Throw the shuttle with your left hand, etc. • Repeat 10 times.	Watch for symmetry, pay attention to how hard you are beating, strive for it feeling the same between right and left throughout the movement. Can you achieve a dance? Would another piece of music work better?
10	Attempt to achieve the same steady rhythm while actually weaving with a loaded shuttle.	

While a regularly timed beat is going to be challenging, if not impossible, when you are following a complicated pattern, becoming aware of your rhythmic movements and the position of your body as you weave can only help you avoid injury and create regularity in your cloth.

Exercises

The first exercise uses a musical piece from YouTube. Feel free to substitute any musical number that has been interpreted by more than one artist. In order to keep the exercises to thirty minute each, the sharing time has been cut down to thirteen minutes in 4.1. But you are encouraged to include additional time to share, if it is available.

Exercise 4.1 (30 minutes)

Twelve Minutes Watch or listen to "Putting It Together" from *Sunday in the Park with George* with Mandy Potemkin on YouTube. Take notice of how Sondheim uses variations in tempo, pitch, volume, rhythm, repetition, and texture to create interest. In your notebook, write down any ideas that may come to you.

Five Minutes Watch or listen to "Putting It Together" sung by Barbara Streisand on YouTube. Take note of how Streisand has used different lyrics that are more relevant to her as a vocalist, rather than a visual artist, without changing the substance of the song. (The sheet music shows "Music and lyrics by Stephen Sondheim" and "Barbra Streisand Version.") In your notebook, write down any ideas that may come to you.

Thirteen Minutes One at a time, share two or three of your ideas from both videos with the group and note any subsequent ideas that come to mind.

Exercise 4.2 (30 minutes)

Ten Minutes Study Figure 4.2 by Tracy Kaestner in this chapter. How might you use this piece as a starting point for your own work?

Twenty Minutes One at a time, share two or three of your ideas with the group and note any subsequent ideas that come to mind.

Conclusion

As you have seen in this chapter, music provides many roads to inspiration for the weaver. Some of the vocabulary of music is familiar to us weavers, including beat, rhythm, tension, and harmony. The issues around copyright and creative borrowing in music help us comprehend the ethics within our own community of weavers. Music can inspire you simply by putting your mind in a creative state, it can help regulate your movements as you weave, and sheet music can more specifically be a jumping off point for a design. If nothing else, weaving can be a fine excuse to spend time with whatever music most touches your soul.

Further Resources for Inspiration

Horowitz, Mark Eden, Sondheim on Music: Minor Details and Major Decisions. Second Edition. Lanham, Maryland: Scarecrow Press, 2010.

"Know Your Rights; Copyright 101 for Weavers." *Weaving Today*, 2012.

Onlinedrummer.com (drum notations)

http://*Sheetmusicdirect.us*

Stephen Sondheim, *Finishing the Hat.* New York: Alfred A. Knopf, 2010.

Stim, Richard. *Getting Permission: How to License & Clear Copyrighted Materials Online & Off,* 5th Edition. Berkeley, California: Nolo, 2013.

MEETING FIVE: BUILDING ART INTO YOUR CRAFT

In this chapter you will learn about architecture, including its design elements, aesthetics, a few of its practitioners, and how the art form might inspire your weaving. We will explore how individual architects, as well as weavers, reside somewhere on a continuum with inspired Art on one end and traditional utilitarian craft on the other. Open and Focused Creativity comes into this discussion as well.

We will also review proportion again, but this time we will explore a more recent theory called the Natural Scaling Hierarchy proposed by mathematician and architectural theorist Nikos Salingaros. His approach provides one of many methods for ensuring that the various elements within a building are scaled closer to nature and thus making a space more comfortable to its inhabitants. His ideas provide interesting possibilities for weaving design as well.

We will consider the work of a few important late 19th and 20th Century architects, such as Julia Morgan, Frank Gehry, Bruce Goff, Ludwig Mies van der Rohe, and Antoni Gaudi, and how they fit into the art versus craft continuum. All have been selected, not for being well known, but for what they can teach us about creativity.

A Very Brief History of Architecture

The definition of architecture that we will use here is the contemporary one, which leans more toward the art of designing buildings and the artistic vision of the architect. The important words in here are "art" and "artistic vision." Without that vision, a structure is merely a building and its designer is merely a builder.

Most of us live and do business in what are considered "vernacular" buildings, conceived for function within a local tradition and with no artistic intention. The first human structures would likely fit within the vernacular.

Figure 5.1 Herders' three-sided shelter. Near Yadi, Bhutan, 2005. Photograph by Larry Stuebing.

One version of the budding of human development can be found in the work of Gottfried Semper (German, 1803-1879), an architect and historian, who in 1851 wrote in *The Four Elements of Architecture* that architectural form arose out of the concepts of the hearth, roof, enclosure, and mound. He believed that the enclosure started off as woven and braided mats of bast and wicker hung vertically to define property and protect the inhabitants from the weather. Such a technique can be found in the shelters used by herders in Bhutan to this day.

These room dividers evolved into the advanced woven tapestries of the ancient Assyrians and Persians. Eventually solid walls began to be placed for support behind the tapestries,

Innovative Weaving

but it was the weaving that was most important to define the enclosure. Eventually the walls began to imitate the look of the tapestries with lots of color and texture that suggested weaving, followed, of course, by plain walls as background for paintings on canvas. Most of Semper's theories have fallen by the wayside, but we weavers can cherish his argument that weaving held a pivotal role in architectural history until someone proves it wrong.

Through much of architectural history, designers of buildings were considered craftsmen with engineering skills, their names usually unrecorded. However, by the time of the Greeks and Romans, they needed to follow well-defined rules for proportions when designing monumental buildings, such as temples. Vitruvius (Roman, c. 80-70 BC to c. 15 BC) wrote *The Ten Books of Architecture*, the only surviving major book on architecture from the classical period. He wrote that a structure must show three qualities: solidity, usefulness, and beauty.

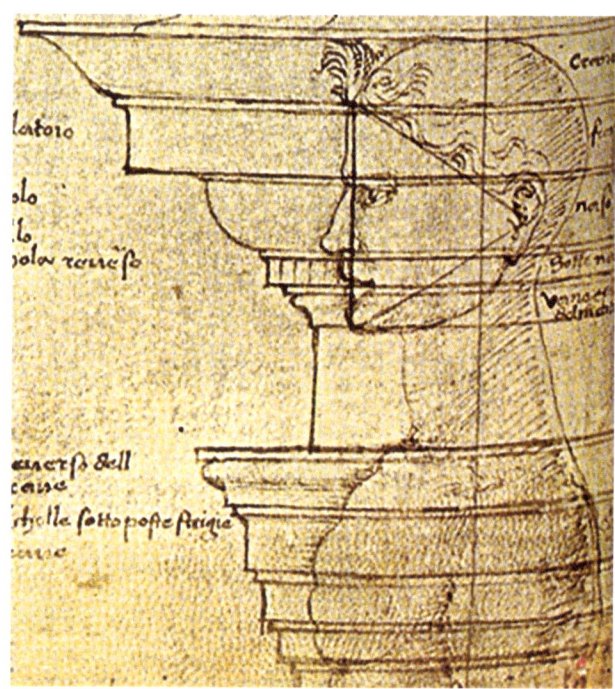

Figure 5.2 Cornice and Vitruvian Man, Francesco di Giorgio. From Trattato di architettura di Francesco di Giorgio Martini, 1475-1495.

Vitruvius also related the Greek architectural orders--Doric, Ionic and Corinthian--to proportions in nature. He developed the concept of what is now called the Vitruvian Man. Leonardo da Vinci illustrated his ideas in a Renaissance edition of Vitruvius' book. The human body, with arms and legs outstretched, are inscribed with the circle and a square to show the perfection of nature's proportions and thus its relevance to architecture.

Before the Renaissance, innovative masterpieces such as Notre-Dame de Paris, considered one of the best examples of Gothic architecture, were attributed only to the "builders," usually the bishops in charge of the funding at the time. But in the Renaissance, creative geniuses, such as Michelangelo Buonarroti (Italian, 1475-1564) and Filippo Brunnellschi (Italian, 1377-1446), were given credit for their architectural skills, as well as in their masterworks in painting and sculpture.

By the end of the 19th Century, architects participated in an explosive period for Art in its many forms. In France there was Art Nouveau and its expression in Spain, particularly in Barcelona, called Modernismo, exemplified by the work of Antoni Gaudi (Catalan, 1852-1926). The 20th Century brought the American Craftsman styles of Julia Morgan (American, 1872-1957) and the Prairie School variation lead by Frank Lloyd Wright (American, 1867-1959), followed by Modernism and Internationalist architects like Ludwig Mies van der Rohe. Architecture in the 21st century continues to evolve as a medium for creative expression as we will explore later in the chapter.

Applying Architectural Formal Elements to Weaving

Architectural design uses many of the same basic visual elements that we have explored in painting and sculpture, such as line, shape, color, texture, and contrasts in light. When these are combined and arranged into units they become part of an architectural composition or formal design. You can

Meeting Five: Building Art into Your Craft

see more examples of the architectural elements as defined by Dr. Harry S. Broudy (Polish, 1905-1998) at the architeacher.org website. He breaks down the formal elements of architecture as follows:

Symmetry/Asymmetry

The contrast between symmetry and asymmetry is easily seen when we compare the regularity of the Beaux Arts New York Public Library to the variability of the Guggenheim Museum in Spain. (See Figure 5.9.) Gaudi's work provides us the following examples:

Figure 5.3 Carrere and Hastings, New York Public Library, 1911, New York City, NY.

Reflection

The mirror image called Reflection Symmetry is seen in these broken tiles in Gaudi's Park Güell.

Figure 5.4 Detail of bench. Antoni Gaudi, Park Güell, Barcelona, Spain, 1900-1914.

Rotational

Rotational Symmetry is the repetition of a shape, but rotated from a fixed point. Note how the palm motif in Gaudi's fencing is repeated in one direction on the top row and then rotated 180 degrees in the bottom row.

Figure 5.5 Detail of fence. Antoni Gaudi, Park Güell, Barcelona, Spain, 1900-1914.

Translation

Translation Symmetry uses a shape copied without change along a straight line. The parabolic arch was a construction innovation of Gaudi's, which he used at a tilt in this Park Güell passageway. The parabolic arch is now considered the most structurally sound of all the arches.

Figure 5.6. Passageway. Antoni Gaudi, Park Güell, Barcelona, Spain, 1900-1914.

Innovative Weaving

Glide Reflection

A shape first reflected to its mirror image and then advanced along a line, such as a set of footprints, is Glide Reflection symmetry. Note how these stylized leaves on this spire are reversed to the opposite side of the stem and shifted up a notch.

Figure 5.7 Detail of spire. Antoni Gaudi, Temple of the Sagrada Família, Barcelona, Spain, 1914.

These variations in architectural symmetry can obviously be used also in our weaving to good effect. Some of them will require more shafts than others, but it is worth exploring how you might create more interest by using vertical borders that use reflection symmetry or rotate a motif. WSSA member Linda Yeatts used translation symmetry in a shawl that was inspired by the capitals on Ionic and Corinthian columns. Textured yarns create even more dimension.

Yeatts usually includes a story with her shawls. This one is about Electra, who served as an Oracle of Delphia or a Pythia. By inhaling vapors, she was able to foretell the future. In Yeatts' version of the story, she really wanted to study architecture, but her family chose her profession instead. Boy, was she pythed!!!

Figure 5.8 Linda Yeatts, *Layers of Architcture*. 2015. Organic cottons.

Balance

While we looked at balance in the sculpture chapter as it related to the physical forces as much as the visual effect, in architecture we are more concerned with the visual balance. We assume the physical balance has been ensured by the architectural engineers. Bilbao's Guggenheim Museum by Frank Gehry (Canada, b. 1929) is a fine example of a well-balanced design. But how did he achieve that effect considering it is such a complex and asymmetrical building? Note how the large vertical masses to the right seem to be balanced by the long low masses to the left. All of this variation would not have been possible before computerized design.

Meeting Five: Building Art into Your Craft

Figure 5.9 Frank Gehry, Guggenheim Museum, Bilbao, Spain, 1997.

WSSA Member Bob Bateman used double weave to create a cityscape. Not seen in the detail in Figure 5.10 is his little red wrecking ball and hook on a beam supporting the hanging and vertical tubing at the bottom, representing sewer pipes.

Of significance here is how Bateman used asymmetry to balance his buildings. The shorter buildings to the left have larger windows that balance the weight of the taller mass of skyscrapers on the right.

Figure 5.10 Bob Bateman. *Cityscape.* Cotton, metal. 2015. Courtesy of the artist.

Pattern and Rhythm

Establishing a repetitive pattern in a controlled rhythm helps attract the eye and control its movement along a piece. Like goddesses across the frieze of a Greek temple, the out-of-work men in Figure 5.11 line up for relief during the Great Depression as part of the Franklin Delano Roosevelt Memorial, Washington, DC, designed by the landscape architect, Lawrence Halprin (American, 1916-2009). The backdrop of the brick wall provides a rather rough pattern, which contrasts with the repeated shiny bronze hat brims and drooping overcoats. The men seem to lean forward, which creates a sense of movement, despite them standing in a wearily static line.

Figure 5.11 Lawrence Halprin, Franklin Delano Roosevelt Memorial, Washington, DC, 1997.

It is easy for weavers to create a pattern. The challenge is to effectively control its rhythm and provide contrast that plays up the desired highlights.

59

Innovative Weaving

Proportion and Scale

While architectural students are taught that Euclid (Greek, mid 4th C-mid 3rd C) wrote of the Golden Ratio of 1.618, there continues to be disagreement as to whether that proportional system was actually used in ancient Greek buildings, such as the Parthenon. However, most agree that proportional formulas definitely governed the Classical orders from the Tuscans on. Jump ahead to the time of Leonardo Fibonacci (Pisa, c.1170-c.1240), who popularized the Hindu-Arabic numeral system in the Western world and also introduced the system of proportions we now call the Fibonacci sequence (1,1,2,3,5,8,13,21, etc.), known to East Indian mathematicians by the 6th Century. While Fibonacci originally used the series of numbers to calculate rabbit population growth, artists continue to use the numbers to help build pleasing proportions in their designs.

One of the pioneers of Modernism, Le Corbusier (French, 1887-1965) developed his own system based on the Golden Ratio, human proportions, and the Fibonnaci sequence, which he called the Modulor. However, like other Modernists, Le Corbusier built his designs by using only a few of the sizes within the sequence, rather than the whole progression.

Nikos Salingaros (Australia, b. 1952) says in his book *A Theory of Architecture* that we are innately uncomfortable when there is not a more natural transition from one size in the scale to the next. Humans need to see transitions of scale from the smallest to the largest in order to feel at ease within a building. He sees many of the Modernist buildings as failing to develop a scale of elements that references the natural world, thus humans find themselves threatened and stressed when they work or play within them.

Salingaros expands upon the work of architect Christopher Alexander, who examined proportion in natural structures, biological forms, and buildings and proposed that a number between two and three was a more natural ratio of the parts than the Golden Ratio or Fibonnaci sequence. Salingaros refined the scaling ratio to 2.7. When scaling the elements in a building, such as windows and other visual divisions, he says that a sequence, such as the Golden Ratio of 1.618, is too small for humans to easily distinguish. Instead a change of 2.7 or rounded to 3 is more perceptible and closer to nature.

This system of scaling has interesting possibilities for weaving design. We will explore the theory in possibilities for weaving more in the Coherence and Using the Natural Scaling Hierarchy in Weaving sections to follow.

Contrast

Contrast in design highlights particular elements and helps us appreciate their differences, such as the glass pyramidal entrance to the Louvre in Paris by I.M. Pei (China, b. 1917). The French Renaissance detailing of the old Louvre palace provides an intriguing contrast to the geometric glass and metal simplicity of the contemporary Pyramid.

Figure 5.12 The Louvre Museum, with I.M. Pei Pyramid entrance, Paris, France, 1982. Public domain image.

Meeting Five: Building Art into Your Craft

Figure 5.13 Bruce Goff, Bavinger House, near Norman, Oklahoma, 1950. Photograph Jones2jy licensed under CC BY 2.0

Another example of the use of contrast in materials is found in the Bavinger House, by Bruce Goff (American, 1904-1982). Much of the ground level walls are made from rough "iron rock" sandstone from nearby quarries. Interspersed within the walls, to both let in light and create contrast, are large chunks of recycled blue-green glass cullets.

Variance in the properties and colors of different yarns is certainly an opportunity to create effective contrast in our weaving. Contrasts in styles could also be fun to play with, such as updating a traditional pattern by using an exaggerated large scale or contemporary colors.

Theme and Variation

In order for architecture to be considered Art, it must have a theme that makes a statement of some kind. Without an artistic statement it is a mere functional building. On the other hand, the theme shouldn't be as restrictive as a prison or it may end up looking like (hmm) a prison. Variations in the theme not only make the work more interesting, but they show the intellectual awareness and originality of the architect.

Frank Gehry's Peter B. Lewis Building provides an intriguing look at how the theme of undulating stainless steel is made even more interesting as it plays off the more geometric and rigid brick and window glass. But wait, the brick and glass windows also bend inward, looking unbelievably as malleable as the metal. The Lewis Building shows how you can have vastly different elements in one project, as long as you find a way to link them together, to show the viewer that these things work together despite their apparent differences.

Figure 5.14 Frank Gehry, Peter B. Lewis Building, Case Western Reserve University, Cleveland, Ohio, 2002. Photograph Harmanani licensed under CC BY SA3.0.

Coherence

In order for a building to be aesthetically successful, all the elements must somehow appear to belong together. Referencing the vocabulary of a particular style of architecture certainly provides one aspect of coherence. Another aspect of coherence is the scale of all the elements within a

Innovative Weaving

building and how they relate to each other. The following rules for achieving coherence within a building design as defined by Salingaros and based on the ratio of 2.7, seem to also be appropriate for a weaving design.

- Define recognizable units through contrast in color and geometry at all scales in the natural scaling hierarchy.

- Tie the different units together through symmetry, overlapping designs, a common grid, complementary shapes, or matching colors.

- Every unit needs a thick boundary (frame) that is itself a unit on the next-smallest scale—sequential units should couple visually with adjoining units.

- Units of different size can link with one another by having a similar shape, so the same pattern repeats at different magnifications.

- Similar patterns of decreasing size can be nested to define a geometrical focus, and this should coincide with a functional focus.

Consider the Natural Scaling Hierarchy, the Golden Mean, or Fibonacci as a jumping off point for your exploration of cohesion in your work. But in the end, trust your own sense to tell you when it all hangs together.

Unity in Variety

In order for a building to appear successful it needs to show a logical unity of its various elements. Consider the antithesis of the Modernist aesthetic in a Balinese Hindu temple. Despite the enthusiastic display of ornate religious figures and motifs, unity is established with the consistent use of light grey. Symmetry also unifies the elements.

Throughout our weaving, we must ensure that the elements appear to belong together. Not in a monotonous way at all, but through a unity of color, texture, patterning, or other design element. Trust your Open Creativity to help you work through challenges such as this, and out of it will come the expression of your individual voice.

Figure 5.15 Hindu Temple, Ubud, Bali, Indonesia.

Function

While not a formal element of architecture as defined by Dr. Broudy, we can't leave out function, which is the most important aspect of any building and where the architect starts. "Form follows function" was the mantra of the Modernist, who wanted to set aside historical styles, particularly ornamentation, and design with the building's use in mind.

Meeting Five: Building Art into Your Craft

While we may feel something disquieting about the spare cold look of the Superdome in New Orleans, we can really only begin to understand modern architecture when we attempt to understand the intentions of its architect. Arthur Q. Davis (American, 1920-2011), along with his partner, Nathaniel Curtis, Jr. (American, 1917-1997) specialized in Modernism in New Orleans, which treasured its 18th century French and Spanish colonial buildings. Davis was trained by Walter Gropius, from the Bauhaus, and Eero Saarinen, designer of Dulles Airport, the St. Louis Arch, and other Modernist works. Curtis defined Modernism as simply a building of its time, using the new materials and techniques currently available, without a need to reference the past.

Figure 5.16 Curtis and Davis, Louisiana Superdome, New Orleans, LA, 1975.

The Superdome clearly represented that approach and was a major achievement for its time, with one of the largest rooms in the world, and with no obstructive supports. Davis was proud of the fact that it was a flexible space, not intended for just one sport or event, but could accommodate many different configurations. Of course, its flexibility was challenged when it became a refuge after the Katrina hurricane in 2005.

The Superdome's exterior form was determined by its function as an environmentally controlled space for the enjoyment of sports and other large events. And it is still being used successfully forty years after its opening. The Modernists would say that whether we find it to our taste or not is immaterial.

A less success building might be the Martin Luther King Jr. Public Library in Washington, DC, by Ludwig Mies van der Rohe (German-American, 1886-1969). This was his last building and his only library. It has to be one of the least user-friendly libraries ever built.

Patrons must walk across large open spaces and ride up and down elevators that are hard to find to get from one book room to another. Way finding is a problem throughout the building. The city continues to explore ways to update the building, while also respecting the iconic architect and his work.

Figure 5.17 Ludwig Mies van der Rohe, Martin Luther King, Jr. Public Library, Washington, DC, 1972.

And so with weaving, a tea towel is not really a tea towel if it doesn't absorb water. Like an architect, we must start with the function and our design and form should come.

Innovative Weaving

Client Relationship

Client relationship is another aspect of architecture that does not fall into Broudy's formal elements, but is essential to the understanding of the Art. The stories of well-known architects and their relationships with their clients is one of the intriguing aspects of architecture. Some architects, like Bruce Goff, Julia Morgan, and Antoni Gaudi, who we will discuss more in the next section, were all about meeting the needs of their clients. Their original designs came out of the attempt to satisfy their clients requests in an artistic manner. Despite his enormous creativity, Bruce Goff said that he never built a house that he would actually live in, but he made his clients happy.

Some architects, driven to express their own theories and vision, without the need to negotiate with a client, built projects just for themselves. such as the Philip Johnson Glass House, 1949. Terunobu Fujimori (Japanese, b. 1946) built an unbelievable teahouse ("Takasugi-An" or "Too Tall Tree House") for his own use that sits on two trees that will even sway in the wind.

But architects usually depend upon the resources and good relationships with their clients. Those that embrace the vision of their patrons have been known to soar to heights otherwise impossible, such as Michelangelo supported by various popes, Julie Morgan and William Randolph Hearst, and Antoni Gaudi and Count Eusebi Güell.

While as weavers we may resist taking on a commission in order to avoid the limitations imposed by a client and thus continue to pursue our art, many fiber artists find that the requirements of a commission can lead to innovative ideas and exploration of new techniques and materials. Obviously a commission depends upon a lot of factors, but it could be an opening for your creativity that takes you into exciting new directions, incorporating client expectations that you might not have otherwise considered important.

Figure 5.18 Terunobu Fujimori, Takasugi-An, Nagano, Japan, 2004. Photograph Dana & LeRoy CC by 2.0.

Is an Architect an Artist or a Craftsperson?

The difference between an artist and a craftsperson has little importance to most people. But the distinction is essential for a young person choosing an educational path toward a career in architecture, for a person of means choosing someone to design their home, and for a weaver to prepare their work for acceptance into an art gallery. And then there are some of us who are just curious about what makes any work Art with a capital "A" and any person an Artist.

Possibly we can think of an Artist and a Craftsperson as being at two ends of a continuum. One end is the ultimate Craftperson, well-skilled at making functional objects by hand using the techniques and materials specific to a tradition shared by other craftspeople.

At the other end of the continuum is the Artist who makes objects or other forms of expression that have no functional use by design. An Artist expresses emotion or possibly a lack of emotion, but is primarily exploring what has not been done before. A chair intentionally impossible to sit in, an origami paper pot, and a shawl made of nails falls closer to Art than Craft. The assumption is that creativity appears more in Art, than it does in Craft. However we know that Open Creativity is

Meeting Five: Building Art into Your Craft

needed anytime we are making something, as challenges arise with new or different materials or processes. And we know that our technical skills as a handweaver require us to use our Focused Creativity to actually produce the work as we imagined.

Determining where a professional architect fits into this imaginary continuum seems to be more complicated. The architect is the idea person, who often has at least one draftsperson put the details of his idea on paper or in computer-aided design (CAD) software, and skilled craftspeople follow through with the architect's vision. Depending upon the complexity of the building and its use of new materials or techniques, a structural engineer might review the plans, using Focused Creativity to ensure the viability of the project. A possible analogy is the apparel designer, who develops a new plaid for the Fall season, a CAD operator then prepares the design for an industrial loom, and the loom operator and the industrial loom create the product according to the specifications of the designer. Both fashion designers and architects work as part of a team, their job requiring that they excel in Open Creativity. While they should understand the importance of craftsmanship, the actual skills are carried out by other members of the team.

In fact, architecture is really primarily concerned with the aesthetics of buildings. The collection of important buildings referred to as the canon of architecture taught in architecture schools includes those unique buildings that are considered innovative, aesthetically or structurally. On the other hand, vernacular buildings, like most houses and commercial buildings, are also studied as a source of a vocabulary for inspiration.

Figure 5.19 Julia Morgan, Hearst Castle, San Simeon, CA, 1919-1947. Public domain photo.

As the first woman architect to have her own practice, Julia Morgan seems to have been too often relegated to the craftsman end of the Artist/ Craftsperson continuum. Morgan designed and supervised the construction of Hearst Castle (1919-1947) at San Simeon, CA for William Randolph Hearst. As a student of Bernard Maybeck, she was steeped in the environmentally sensitive San Francisco Bay Area version of the Arts and Craft style, called the First Bay Tradition style, Morgan clearly knew how to meet or exceed the requirements of her customers, as witnessed by her legacy of 750 buildings, more than any other major architect of her time. She also designed sixteen structures for Asilomar in Pacific Grove, built for the YWCA. Morgan used local materials and integrated her buildings into their coastal pine environment.

Morgan was trained as an engineer at the University of California at Berkeley and then received an architectural degree from Ecole des Beaux-Arts in Paris. As a practicing and independent architect she was highly respected for her structural expertise. However she did not write about her work and didn't like to be interviewed. Therefore the intellectual side of her work is not available for the academics. In 2006, when the de Young Museum presented an exhibit of California architects in the Arts and Crafts movement, Julia Morgan was not included, despite the fact that she had designed over 200 public and private buildings in the style. When challenged about her absence from the exhibit while architects of similar aesthetic, such as Maybeck and Greene and Greene were included, the curators said she was only on the fringes of the movement. While we can argue as to whether she was more an artist or a craftsperson, clearly in the eyes of these curators she was too much the latter.

Innovative Weaving

Gaudi is an example of an exceptionally innovative architect. While we do know that he was driven to interpret the natural world of God within the language of his Catalan heritage, he, like Morgan, did not write or talk about his work. He came from four generations of craftsmen metalworkers. Gaudi provided a good blend of craft skills and originality in many buildings that continue to stand out as odd and unusual to the modern viewer, as they did to his contemporaries.

Bruce Goff is a lesser-known architect that meets the definition of an architect on the Art side of the continuum for several reasons. First, he taught at the University of Oklahoma in Norman, thus giving him some academic credibility, access to other thinkers about his own field and others, and the forum to expound on his theories. Second, he designed buildings that were undisputably original, such as the Bavinger House. Third, there are several books on his work, including one of interviews and lectures. Thus his theories on environmentally sensitive architecture and creativity are available to be passed down to future architects. He was particularly inspired by the concept of the "continuous present," where no project has a beginning or an end. A building didn't spontaneously come about, and it will have a life long after the completion of construction.

Figure 5.20 Antoni Gaudi, Casa Batllo, Barcelona, Spain, 1906

However Goff's works are less well-known because his commissions were not major public or corporate buildings, but instead were private homes, small churches, and small commercial buildings, mostly in Oklahoma. But Goff had a strong imagination, along with the desire to help his clients meet their own visions, financial budgets, and functional requirements.

In our weaving world, we also recognize who is more an Artist and who is more a Craftsperson. We know the makers of mass-produced, machine-made functional tea towels are not performing as either Artists or Craftspeople. We know those few members in our guild who always seem to come up with ideas that are off-the-wall original. They are our Artists. And we are in awe of those members that excel at exquisite craftsmanship. What about the rest of us?

Do you see yourself as more a Craftsperson on the continuum, enjoying perfecting time-honored techniques using traditional patterns and materials? Or do you have a need to make a personal statement about the world or your inner feelings using materials in unexpected ways with techniques you developed yourself? Likely you are somewhere in between these extremes, as a Craftsperson depending upon Focused Creativity to best express and pass on the traditions of weaving or as an Artist using the power of Open Creativity to innovate and develop a unique body of work.

The only thing that is important about where you see yourself right now on the Artist/Craftsperson continuum is that it is where you want to be. If you would like to be more one way or the other, take some time to consider classes you could take to improve your technical or artistic skills. How about simply stretching yourself one way or the other on your next project. You get to choose how you see yourself now and into the future as an Artist, an artistic craftsperson, a skilled artist, or a skilled Craftsperson.

Meeting Five: Building Art into Your Craft

Using the Natural Scaling Hierarchy in Weaving

Nikos Salingaros has not only applied his theory on proportion and coherence to architecture, but also to oriental rugs. You are encouraged to search for "The Life of a Carpet" by Salingaros on the web to learn more about his approach to design. His book *A Theory of Architecture* may be rather technical, but has so much that we can apply to our own designs. Some of the points that are most relevant to our work are the following:

- Choose only one measurement for calculating the hierarchy throughout, such the length, the width, or the area.

- An example of a natural scaling sequence for a weaving piece based on the ratio of 3 (2.7 rounded) would be .25in, .75in, 2.25in, 6.75in, and a final width of 20.25 inches.

- You can start with the smallest factor and multiply by 3 or start with the final length or width and divide by 3 to get each size in the sequence.

- The smaller the unit the more you use in a repetition. Fewer are used as the scale gets bigger.

- Don't feel trapped by a specific size in the sequence, close is good enough.

- Use repetition to highlight the element.

- The smallest unit on the hierarchy should be the smallest you can see from a comfortable distance. Thus it may be each warp and weft threads in 5/2 cotton.

Exercises

The following exercises encourage you to think about the place of architecture in your life and how it has influenced your personal aesthetic.

Exercise 4.1 (30 minutes)

Ten Minutes Is there a particular architectural style that appeals most to you? How has that influenced your weaving?

Twenty Minutes Share your thoughts with the group and note any subsequent ideas that come to mind.

Exercise 3.2 (30 minutes)

Ten Minutes What building in the whole world, according to your own aesthetic, do you find most appealing? What could you make for its decor that would be appropriate for its style and function? Write down as many ideas as you can think of and elaborate on those that most interest you.

Twenty Minutes Tell the group what your chosen building is, why you love it, and what one or two items you can imagine making for it.

Innovative Weaving

Conclusion

Architecture provides us an opportunity to reflect on the importance of developing and drawing from our technical skills as well as nurturing our creative imaginations. We also can discover new approaches to design from architectural theory, such as the Natural Scaling Hierarchy. Most of all we need to keep our eyes open as we pass through our cities and towns, paying attention to architectural patterns and proportions, along with new and old styles, that may provide inspiration for our own work.

Further Resources for Inspiration

Architizer.com for architectural award winners

Search "Gaudi textiles" in Google Image

ritzkerprize.com for architectural awards

MEETING SIX: LET'S PUT ON A SHOW!

In this chapter we explore Performance Art, a live event that is all about the moment, where nothing is made to be sold. The performance is rarely repeated or recorded except in the memory of the people there. While performance art may seem the antithesis of weaving, it provides an opportunity to look at collaboration and how your guild might develop a performance that engages the community and introduces the public to the organization and the inventiveness of weavers.

Even if you don't have an opportunity to develop a guild performance, this chapter encourages you to collaborate with one or more friends to expand the skills you have available and to take advantage of your group brainstorming skills to generate and evaluate innovative ideas.

As a disclaimer, Performance Art can be very dark when it uses violence and heavily sexual content to shock and make political or other emotionally charged statements. In this chapter, we are exploring only the G-rated version. You will find a couple of references at the end of the chapter that more thoroughly explore the history of Performance Art and the intentions of the creative geniuses expressing themselves through the art form.

A Very Brief History of Performance Art

How about this for a definition? Performance art is live art by artists. Any more restrictive definition seems to leave out elements of this open-ended art form. We could say that Leonardo da Vinci was expressing himself through performance when he dressed people as planets in 1490 and had them recite verses about the Golden Age. Another precursor occurred in 1909 when the Futurists acted out a parable of warfare where the digestive system represented the battle between the eaters and the eaten.

Dadaists, Surrealists, and Bauhaus artists all used performance to express their concerns about art and politics. But the real beginning of performance art is considered to be the first "happening" at Black Mountain College, North Carolina, in 1952, when John Cage created what was later titled *Theatre Piece No. 1* and put it on the same day. It incorporated music, dance, spoken word, projections, and other visual art. There was no division between a stage and the audience, no definite length. No plot, just a sparse script. All was left to chance.

By 1968, Conceptualists were striving for an art form where there was no actual object that could be bought and sold. Performance was an extension of that idea, often breaking down the barriers between performers and audience. The experience of time, space, and ideas was the importance, rather than any resulting object.

Some might say that the jam band the Grateful Dead and their participatory audience of devoted Deadheads represent performance art. Their rhythm guitarist, Bob Weir, revels in the time they were "One with the music; one with the audience." Every concert was an improvisation, with no song ever played the same way.

Innovative Weaving

Five Collaborative Performance Artists

While not all performance artists want the viewer to participate in their work, many do see audience involvement as vital to their creative expression. This collaboration, often spontaneous, is an important element in the work of the following artists:

Anna Halprin (American, b. 1920)

Early in her career as a traditionally trained dancer, Anna Halprin became interested in improvisational movement "to find out what our bodies could do, not learning somebody else's pattern or technique." She believed movement should not be restricted by music or even just interpreting ideas.

Halprin formed the San Francisco Dancer's Workshop in 1959 with other dancers and the artists John Cage and Robert Morris. Their mission was to delve into explorative forms of dance and away from the technical constraints of modern dance. They wanted to move freely with emotion and with a feeling of community.

After a bout with colon cancer in 1971, Halprin dedicated her efforts to healing, as well as social and political issues, through dance. At some point, she decided that she wasn't dancing to entertain and wanted viewers to participate, rather than just watch.

As of 2015, Anna Halprin at 95 continues to lead an annual participatory dance in Mt. Tamalpais State Park, north of San Francisco. The Planetary Dance is a free all-day ritual of "healing, peace, and community renewal." The participants form into concentric circles with drums helping to coordinate their movements.

Yoko Ono (Japan, b. 1933)

While we may know Yoko Ono mostly for her role in breaking up the Beatles, she was expressing herself through performance art before she met John Lennon. Ono performed *Cut Piece* by sitting center stage with her legs tucked under her. She invited audience members to cut off pieces of her clothing. In 2003, she performed it again in Paris saying that this is "a time where we need to trust each other."

A more well-known performance work is *Bed-In for Peace* where John Lennon and Ono sat in bed surrounded by the press for their 1969 honeymoon.

Franz Erhard Walther (Germany, b. 1939)

One of the first artists in Europe to explore performance art was Franz Erhard Walther. Always an artist wanting to experiment with new expression, by the early 1960s Walther was exploring space, time, and viewer participation. He liked working with plain cotton fabrics and seeing what happens when you add the element of time.

In 1963, he came upon a tailor's ham used to iron curved seams. The idea hit him that he could sew, rather than glue, pieces of fabric together. He called it "A historically untapped artistic method." As fiber artists, such a revelation seems odd. But it was 1963, and he felt it necessary to distance his work from the mundane. Walther writes:

> In order to remain within the realm of art...I employed terms such as sculpture, proportion, volume, dimension, temporal articulation, place, inside, outside, pedestal, covering, direction, concentration, duration, space, body, dimension, distance, relation, opposite, place to stand, movement.

His performance pieces consist of three elements: the storage form, the demonstration of how to use the piece, and the action itself. One typical example, from 1966, consists of two plain white strips of fabric about 20 feet long and 5 feet wide, sewn together to create five large pockets. For the performance, the piece is laid flat on the floor. Five participants stand at the open end. They then enter the pockets, lying on their backs. A sculptural, yet living, effect is created. Another piece created in 1967, called *Going On* had twenty-eight pockets sewn into a long length of fabric laid out in a field. Four people moved from one pocket to the next, causing the fabric to take on a continually evolving sculptural shape. As recent as 2014, his work was exhibited at WIELS Contemporary Art Centre in Brussels. People were encouraged to come to training sessions where they would learn to perform in his *First Works Set* (1963-69).

Marina Abromović (Serbia, b. 1946)

Marina Abromović began exploring performance and body art in the early 1970s. Her work examines the artist's ability to confront pain, blood, and her physical limits. Scary, huh? She is also interested in the relationship between the performer and the audience.

Abromović performed one of her tamer pieces *Breathing In/Breathing Out* with her then-husband, Ulay, in the mid-1970s. They plugged their noses with cigarette filters, held their mouths together and exhaled breaths for fourteen minutes until they used all the available oxygen and nearly passed out. The concept was around the idea that an individual can absorb the life of someone else, exchanging, and ultimately destroying it. Need I say, do not try this at home.

In 2010, Abromović performed *The Artist is Present*, where she sat silently in a chair for a total of 736½ hours with MOMA visitors taking turn sitting silently across the table from her.

Olaniyi Rasheed Akindiya AKIRASH (Nigeria, b. 1973)

AKIRASH's work explores our struggles with the environment, rampant consumerism, and competition for scarce resources. He sees performance as a more effective way to reach the heart and mind of the audience, than painting, sculpture, or installation. AKIRASH is not afraid to appear as a fool in his live art, because he believes his message will sneak up on the viewers once they are home and have an opportunity to reflect on what they saw.

Figure 6.1 Olaniyi Rasheed Akindiya AKIRASH, *OKEKU (Shields against death)*, Main Street/Main Street Park, Dallas, TX, Febuary 15, 2014. Photo courtesy of ARTWITHAKIRASH.

Innovative Weaving

Collaboration Sparks Creative Ideas

Involvement of the audience is important to the success of much performance art, as we have seen in the work of the five artists discussed above. The desire to participate in collaborative performance art can be seen in to the popularity of events such as Burning Man in Black Rock Desert, Nevada, and regional spin-offs, such as Burning Flipside, outside Austin, Texas.

The "Burning Man" episode of *Malcolm in the Middle* provides a humorous view of the clash between the life of the average suburban father (Bryan Cranston) setting up his RV at a campground and the expectations of the participants at Burning Man. As Hal sets out his family's private space outside the RV, defined by an AstroTurf rug and gas barbecue grill, the "burners" gather around to watch his performance, thoroughly enjoying the irony. The more Hal's frustration rises as he tries to shoo them away, the more people come to laugh and applaud their idea of artistic expression.

The *Survival Guide* for Burning Flipside describes the event as a place for participants to "create art, performance, and social space on a larger scale than one person could alone." The guide insists that there are no observers, only participants.

No money is exchanged at Flipside, except for ice, creating a "gift economy." One camp group provides a costume tent where participants can sort through racks filled with everything from satin, sequined ball gowns to robot costumes. Most people walk out with big smiles and a new persona. A fashion show provides people an opportunity to create their own one-minute extemporaneous performance, showing off their costumes. In 2015, the fashion show included:

- A dominatrix and a naked man on his haunches with a long white beard and small red fez strapped to his head, clanging little brass cymbals.

- A man in a short satin red dress with a shawl collar that nicely framed the large eagle tattoo on his back.

- "The Almost Good Witch" in a baby blue puffy sleeved, full skirted dress fit for the Wizard of Oz.

- A finely crafted and designed plastic bead dress by Pamela Steel, shown in Figure 6.2. Strings of lights added even more pizzazz.

The Flipside fashion show had minimum structure and no rehearsal. Two announcers shared the microphone and improvised, using just a card with a name of the model, sometimes their fictional burner name, and the piece's title. The models were only required to walk the length of the ground cloth and back. How they used the space and how much time they took was up to them. The most applause, of course, was for those that engaged the crowd in some way. The openness and acceptance of the announcers and the crowd provided the space for the models to freely express themselves through performance.

Figure 6.2. Pamela Steel. Bead woven dress, Flipside, Austin, TX, 2015.

Meeting Six: Let's Put on a Show!

Group Flow in Your Guild

Many of us belong to guilds that regularly demonstrate weaving and spinning for the public. What would happen if we expanded the possibilities of that community interaction by creating a performance that involved many of our members, along with observers. Such an effort might use the brainstorming skills we have been practicing to come up with innovative approaches.

In his book, *Group Genius: The Creative Power of Collaboration*, Keith Sawyer lauds the power of "group flow," which makes each participant more creative and produces results greater than any one person could possibly achieve. In addition to the brainstorming rules we have been using, Sawyer writes that there are conditions that help ensure that group brainstorming efforts result in innovation. They include more Focused Creativity than we normally practice in the Exercises here, such as starting with a specific goal and evaluation of the ideas, because the intention is collaboration, where everyone's ideas contributed to the whole. Conditions for effective group flow include the following:

A clear goal for the group to focus on.

Close listening. Everyone needs to just listen to each other, rather than focusing on one's own ideas.

Being in control. The group needs to feel that the results of their efforts will have an impact, rather than be overturned by a higher power, and that all members will defer to the group's results.

Blending egos. Everyone in the group needs to control their egos and balance their close listening with the contribution of their own ideas. Ideas will merge and lack individual ownership.

Equal participation. No experts should be telling everyone what to do. Experts need to listen like everyone else and accept the authority of the group.

Building on Ideas. Listen to what is being said, accept it, and then build on it.

Acceptance of Risk or Failure. Rather than fearing failure, every activity needs to be thought of as a rehearsal for the next time.

Use of a Facilitator. A facilitator needs to know what organizational format work best for the situation, how to keep the group from getting stuck, and how to ensure everyone contributes.

Switch between group and individual activities. Both are needed to ensure the most innovative ideas are brought out.

Evaluate ideas. One approach for evaluation is to assign points of 1 to 5 according to how unique and different each idea is and then how valuable the idea is socially, artistically, and economically. Exercise 6.1 describes another method for this evaluation.

All of these conditions can help your guild develop innovative ideas for a piece you could perform for the public or at a guild meeting. Perfection shouldn't be the goal. More will be gained if everyone focuses on the moment and embraces the risk and joy of creative collaboration.

Innovative Weaving

Conflict in Collaboration

With creative collaboration naturally comes inevitable disagreements. Creativity is stimulated by these differences, as long as there is a healthy and respectful way to negotiate out of conflict toward a shared goal. Conflict is a quick way to also discover problems that need to be solved. In addition, in the strongest groups, everyone knows how and when to lead and when to follow.

Like in married couples, if the collaborators have many more positive exchanges than negative, then they can be productive. Once there are more negative exchanges than positive, the collaboration becomes ineffective and is unlikely to last. If such a crisis occurs in your group, a review of the list of conditions earlier in this chapter might help get the effort back on track.

Location, Location (or Not)

Collaboration once required artists to live and work in the same large cities, such as New York, Paris, and San Francisco. There artists were able to bounce thoughts off of each other, build on each others ideas, and be inspired by each other's experimentation. Rare are the artists that are able to thrive without the interaction of other artists. Your guild can provide that needed input, critique, and inspiration, along with the networking that comes from attending at regional festivals and national conferences, like the Handweavers Guild of America (HGA) biennial Convergence.

On the other hand, the web now allows us to collaborate with people all over the world. Complex Weavers has online study groups, like Beyond Plain Weave Garments, where you can share designs and images of your work and receive critique. The Yahoo Group WeaveTech provides a "focused, intelligent, and quality dialogue" for weavers with several years experience. Weavolution.com sees itself as "collaborative learning." There is also a support group for people working on HGA's Certificate of Excellence.

However, weavers are far from the level of collaboration on the web that musicians are now enjoying. Through Kompos.com and Splice.com, individual musicians are able to upload their parts of a song in order to create a full orchestration. Possibly one of you will develop a way to expand on the round robin process for the web?

Collaboration in Pairs

You might collaborate on some projects with your guild, but you should also consider partnering with only one other person for your more personal ideas. Joshua Wolf Shenk, in his book *Powers of Two*, makes the case that innovation almost always comes out of collaboration, rather than individual genius, particularly through the creative power of two people. He writes that there are essentially three variations of bonded creative pairs:

Asymmetrical One partner is the leader and the other the disciple or deputy.

Distinct Each partner has a separate public identity, with no collaboration on a specific work, but there is a reliance on each other for inspiration and advice. The fantasy writers C.S. Lewis and J.R.R. Tolkien are an example.

Overt Partners are roughly equal and are publicly known to produce work together. The writing team of John Lennon and Paul McCartney are an example.

Meeting Six: Let's Put on a Show!

The choreographer Merce Cunningham (American, 1919-2009) and composer John Cage (American, 1912-1992) seemed to have a hybrid Distinct/Overt partnership when it came to their joint performances. They created pieces to be performed in the same space and at roughly the same time, but very rarely did the dancers effort and the music come together. Cage says that whenever the curtain came down the music stopped, because people started to applaud.

Collaborating with someone who has skills you don't have can inspire you to attempt work that would otherwise be impossible. The fiber artist Pam Farley has been able to create more complex three-dimensional work because of the ability of her husband, Joe, to engineer appropriate hanging devices. And, if your sewing skills are limited, partnering with a skilled tailor or dressmaker helps ensure your woven yardage looks its best.

WSSA's Performance at a Weaving Conference

In June 2015, WSSA organized the Contemporary Handweavers of Texas biennial conference in Austin. Since our creativity study group was focusing on performance art that month, we took the opportunity to use the brainstorming techniques in the chapter to quickly pull together a performance piece for one of the luncheons.

Some of our members had been writing jokes related to spinning and weaving, such as:

> What do weavers and spinners have that felters don't?
>
> Tension

Figure 6.3. Melinda Estelle, Mickey Stam, Linda MacMillan, and Inga Marie Carmel in WSSA performance during the luncheon at Contemporary Handweavers of Texas Conference, Austin, TX, June 2016.

We used these as a jumping off point. Certainly our performance piece didn't have the artistic seriousness of an Abromović or Ono, but the intention was to practice collaboration and group creativity. The parameters we started with were:

- Performance in 10 days
- No time for rehearsal or memorization
- We would make our own costumes as each of us was inspired
- The jokes the members had been writing would be the core

We brainstormed individually and then I listed the ideas on flipchart sheets that we hung around the room. Everyone had five dots to vote for their favorite. The most popular were:

- An MC to ask the audience if they had question for the robot who knew everything.
- Study group members would be scattered around the audience to raise their hand and read the first part of the joke.
- Robot to read the punch line to the joke.
- Drummer to play a rim shot after each punch line.
- Bodyguard to lead the robot, MC, and drummer into the room, holding the "crowd" back.
- Hat lady in a funny hat to walk behind the MC.

Innovative Weaving

We had a script of the order of the jokes. Everyone knew what to do in what order. It was all perfectly silly, but we had a great time. And best of all it was a group effort.

Exercises

The following exercises help you practice collaborative brainstorming and possibly develop a performance for your group.

Exercise 6.1 (60 minutes)

Ten Minutes Assume your guild has an opportunity for a performance coming up within the next several weeks. List in silence as many ideas that you can come up with for a performance related to weaving, spinning, dyeing, or felting.

Twenty Minutes Share two or three of your ideas. Have one person record each idea on a flip chart.

Fifteen Minutes Vote for three of your favorite ideas using stick-on dots. Consider how unique each one is and how doable it is within the time frame and resources of the group. Feel free to discuss your choices with others as you place your dots.

Fifteen Minutes Facilitator reads off the top vote getters and asks for a consensus vote on the selected ideas. Discuss any concerns and modify ideas, if necessary. Another consensus vote should be taken to determine if the performance is something the group would actually like to do. If it is a go, decide when the group should meet for further development of the ideas.

Conclusion

Performance provides an exciting opportunity for encouraging collaboration and cohesion within your guild. It also provides an opportunity to consider what you would most want to communicate to the public about your guild and its mission. By learning how to work together effectively, listening to each other, and trusting the group, you will be practicing the ability to creatively collaborate on work that is even closer to your heart, your own individual artistic expression.

Further Sources for Inspiration

RoseLee Goldberg. *Performance Art from Futurism to the Present*. 3rd Ed. New York: Thames and Hudson, 2011.

RoseLee Goldberg. *Performance: live art since the 60s.* New York: Thames and Hudson, 2004.

MEETING SEVEN: WEAVE YOUR PASSION

What are those things that get your juices flowing? Is it your family, politics, the environment, your spiritual beliefs, health, or weaving itself? Unless you practice tapestry, double weave pickup, or jacquard, it can be a challenge to represent those passionate ideas in your weaving. In this chapter we will explore how artists, including weavers, have added content to their work in order to touch the hearts and minds of viewers and possibly inspire them to take some sort of action.

Unfortunately we need to consider the Art Snob, who may be the gatekeeper to venues where you would like to show your work. This chapter helps you think about different ways to express yourself and which environments will be most receptive, such as a church bazaar, street craft show, guild show, or art gallery. The more you understand viewer expectations, including that of the Art Snob, the better chance you have for your exhibit application to be accepted.

Many art galleries and exhibitions expect you to have a personal vision or a bigger idea within your work. The artist statement gives you the opportunity to communicate those concepts. This chapter includes many effective examples from contemporary weavers.

A Very Brief History of Artistic Passion

Any artwork or fine craft must have had some sort of passion behind it, whether it was the determination required to chip away a petroglyph in Libya, the religious vision of El Greco, or the pride in the skill to craft a Chippendale chair.

George Catlin (American, 1796-1872) was never considered an innovative painter, but he knew the craft of portraiture and he was driven. His passion was telling the story of the vanishing Native American tribes devastated by whiskey and small pox. Over six years he created 300 studio-style portraits documenting the clothing, hair, makeup, and accouterments of the First Americans. He said "nothing short of the loss of my life, shall prevent me from visiting their country, and of becoming their historian." The passion behind his output, his ability to communicate his concerns in writing, and the validity of his message overcame any limitations that might be seen in his craftsmanship as a painter.

Modernists, like Jackson Pollack (American, 1912-1956), risked acceptance of their work as they developed their own form of expression through abstraction. But with the right contacts in the art world and his ability to talk its language, Pollack was able to achieve wide exposure. He said that abstraction enabled both the direct expression of an "inner world," of individual feeling, and the urgencies and tensions of modern American life represented by "the airplane, the atom bomb, the radio."

Figure 7.1 George Catlin. Ju-ah-kis-gaw, Woman with her Child in a Cradle, 1835. Oil on canvas, 29 x 24 in. Smithsonian American Art Museum, Gift of Mrs. Joseph Harrison, Jr. Courtesy of the museum.

Innovative Weaving

Pollock's most often quoted statement about his methods exemplifies this concern with a creativity arising from the unconscious: "When I am in my painting, I'm not aware of what I'm doing. It is only after a sort of 'get acquainted' period that I see what I have been about." His words, verbal or written, are essential to our understanding of his contribution to art.

Explanation was rarely needed in figurative art, although the academic field of art history is dependent upon chatter about innovative techniques and artistic development. However abstract art is another animal. If we knew nothing about the intention of Jackson Pollack and Mark Rothko (American, 1903-1970) their paintings would be meaningless. Once we understand what they were trying to accomplish and why they chose to do what they did, we can appreciate their innovations within the context of their time.

Finessing the Art Snob

While critics have surely been around since the first image of a bison appeared on a rock face, the more recent version of the Art Snob evolved out of the belief that "Art" is produced only by professional artists trained in an art school. Most often with an art education themselves, possibly even with a Masters in Fine Arts, the Art Snob is steeped in art history and theory, and in the worse form can be derisive of craft in its many forms. An Art Snob may even define serious Art to include only oil painting and sculpture. And, in his or her view, if you don't have the academic art background, you can't be an Artist. As weavers we might not care, except that these prejudices can get in the way of our opportunities to exhibit our work, such as when Art Snobs are gallery owners or exhibition judges. Understanding this narrow point of view provides us an opportunity to examine our own work and consider how we might be able to make small or larger adjustments in our work that might open the minds of these gatekeepers to the innovations in contemporary weaving, thus exposing more people to this craft that we all love.

When Art Snobs, and the average viewer for that matter, first see innovative work, they might not necessarily like it. But if the artist has done a good job of writing some sort of explanation of their intentions, the Art Snob can at least appreciate the work and through time might actually grow to love it.

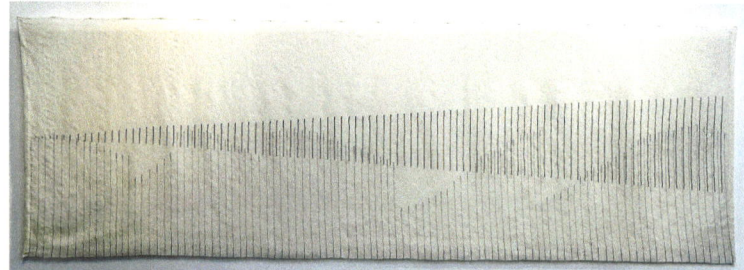

Figure 7.2 Robin Johnston, *Intervals*, 2011. 32 x 100 in. Handwoven cotton. Courtesy of the artist.

The work of Robin Johnston (American, 1979) provides a good example of how understanding the artist's inspiration might help our appreciation of an abstracted weaving. Johnston's passion is the environment and global warming. Her interest in statistics and attention to detail allowed her to tell the story of climate change and its effects of the ocean. She says of *Intervals*:

> My studio at the Headlands was right on the edge of a major city [San Francisco], and sometimes it was hard to feel connected to the ocean and the natural environment even when I was surrounded by it. So I made a series based on daily tide charts from Point Bonita, near the studio. The work illustrates the constant, cyclical tides, and seeks to explore my feelings of distance from the cycle. [It] is intended to represent the underlying fact of a slowly rising sea level, acknowledging the impact human existence has on the earth's natural time rhythms. I would stop weaving every six minutes (which is how often the tide gauge measures) and record the tide height. The waves were created in the tabby weave by using a comb.

Meeting Seven: Weave Your Passion

By communicating her underlying concept, Robin's piece comes alive and allows us to connect to its story. On her website she describes her overall work as follows:

> One goal of my work is to bring a viewer's attention to the quieter side of things, inviting them to look closer into themselves by creating a space for contemplation. However, there is a deeper level of protest in choosing to work in a widely forgotten medium and deliberately making the process of weaving much slower than necessary. My work deals with measuring time, capturing moments as they pass by, and the sense of loss that accompanies their passing.

Through Johnston's ability to articulate her intentions and passion, she turns what appears to be a relatively simple weaving into a work that will grab the attention of many Art Snobs.

Expressing and Sharing Your Passion

Figure 7.3 Detail of Robin Johnston, *Intervals*, 2011. Courtesy of the artist.

We all have something, whether personal, local, or global, that might either obsess us or help us find serenity. Weaving provides a vehicle for sharing those feelings and ideas with others. Say your passion is your black Lab. You could weave a naturalistic portrait in tapestry based on a photo. Your intention is pretty clear, particularly if you title it "My Dog Spot."

You could also take your passion to a more conceptual level. Suppose you volunteer at the Humane Society and are disturbed by puppy mills. You might use that same photo and do a tapestry that shows hundreds of puppies, overlapped and crowded. You could write an artist statement that explains your concerns.

You could also do something completely abstract, possibly black squares, some deformed, and then throw in some red spots. Possibly spin in some of Spot's hair. Then describe your inspiration and concerns about puppy mills in your statement.

Or you could use the same abstract piece, but don't be so specific. Your inspiration might be the same, but give the viewer an opportunity to invent their own interpretation. This time say in the artist statement that you are concerned about how humans lord over other creatures or that you worry about commercialization and how it is destroying all that is valuable in the world.

All of these approaches to your work are valid. But they are only valued in certain environments. It is your passion that is important, the technical skills you bring to interpreting that passion, and finding the best venue for people to see your work and respond to your passion.

Innovative Weaving

Figure 7.4 Mary Macaulay, *Temptation, Sucking the Life Out,* 2007. Felted wool.

While Mary Macaulay (American, 1945), a WSSA member, was reading the novel *The Kite Runner* by Khaled Hosseini that describes the horror of life under the Taliban rule in Afghanistan, she was also working on a pretty felted vessel in her studio. Her response to a particularly terrifying section of the book was to throw the partially completed damp piece around the room in frustration and anger. Out of that came *Temptation, Sucking the Life Out.* (Fig. 7.3) The large parasitic flower is sucking all the life out of the vessel and spider-like forms are accentuating the devastation and violence of the Taliban. Her explanation of the piece's inspiration was a major factor in its ultimate sale.

One of our study group members, Linda Yeatts, weaves lovely shawls that she sells at craft shows. She has found most success when she writes a short clever story on the piece's label, which provides a way for the viewer to connect to her work. See one of her stories accompanying Figure 5.8. Some buyers are motivated to purchase a shawl because they love the story. And sometimes her booth is full of people merely enjoying the labels. Few of us have the skill to write like Yeatts, but her experience demonstrates the importance of words to help viewers connect with the weaver and the work.

It is one thing to weave your passion, then write some words to communicate your inspiration and intention, but then how do you find the right venue to share it? Whether your work has a concept behind it or is purely functional, it can be a challenge to find the right environment.

If you belong to a guild, you likely have opportunities to exhibit and sell any of your work, whether with conceptual or purely functional. But if you want to show your work outside those regular venues, you might run into the gatekeeping Art Snob that treasures painting and sculpture, but has little appreciation of the creative expression possible in weaving.

While this prejudice can be infuriating, as a weaver you have an opportunity to consider Art Snob's opinion and then explore ways you might be able to better meet their expectations. Or you may respect their opinion, find deep satisfaction in the craft of weaving, and be satisfied with your current opportunities to display your work. Either way, there are benefits in understanding the Art Snob's expectations and being aware where one might be lurking, particularly when he/she might get in the way of your personal goals as a weaver.

Recently there was a weaving exhibit where the entry form used "Art," "decorative," and "concept art" to describe the same category. A few highly skilled weavers entered what they saw as purely decorative wall pieces in that category. The judge wrote on their feedback forms that she was unable to judge their work without an artist statement. Their disappointment could have been avoided if the entry form had provided separate categories for wall hangings and concept art, along with making it clear that concept art required an artist statement. The following pages are an attempt to minimize such confusion in terms and thus continue to encourage you to share your work in the most welcoming venues.

Meeting Seven: Weave Your Passion

Fiber Art Categories

Some of the following terms may be loaded with the prejudices of the Art Snob, which includes some art gallery owners and the occasional exhibit judge, but it is a point of view that can help you understand their expectations.

Kitsch   Overly sentimental or garish, possibly in poor taste. Usually mass produced, inexpensive materials, such as plastic.

Crafty   Handmade, quickly made, less expensive materials, lower level of craftsmanship.

Decorative   Ornamental.

Decorative Art   Mass-produced functional objects, such as furniture, china, and silverware.

Functional Craft   Useful and hand made. Includes rugs, dish towels, table linen. Includes traditional design as well as innovative.

Fine Craft   High level of craftsmanship. High quality materials. Innovative. Both functional and nonfunctional. Possibly artistic content.

Wearable Art   Handmade, one-of-a-kind apparel, including scarves and other accessories. The yardage is mostly handwoven or surface manipulated commercial fabric, particularly dyed.

Concept Art   Artistic content or meaning required. Fine craftsmanship is less important, but still appreciated. Likely needs to emulate painting and sculpture by hanging on the wall, possibly within a frame, or standing on its own.

Welcoming Environments

With the understanding of how the Art Snob might categorize your weaving, let's look at the types of environments that are friendly to the different categories.

Your Home	Obviously complete freedom
Church Bazaar	Crafty
Street Craft Fair	Crafty, possibly kitsch
Guild Show	Usually open to whatever you weave
Wearable Art Shop	One of a kind, handcrafted apparel
HGA Convergence	Different categories, but fine craftsmanship is usually required, unless artistic merit overrides it.
Fine Craft Show	Fine craft, often includes concept
Art Gallery	Concept Art

The smaller your town the more chance a gallery will be flexible in what it accepts, combining concept art, wearable art, fine craft, and even some crafty pieces. The larger cities often have enough artists available to be more specialized.

Innovative Weaving

The viewers at each of these environments have different expectations. You are welcome to attempt to exhibit in any of these environments, but your success is going to be more assured if you chose the right venue for your work.

Writing an Artist Statement

While you might not need to write an explanation of your tapestry portrait of "My Dog Spot," the more there is a story behind your weaving and the less figurative it is, the more the viewer needs your guidance through a written artist statement. No need to worry about using any specific terminology or topics that need to be covered. If you are worried about your grammar or spelling, simply have a couple of people edit it for you. As you will see in a few pages, there is a wide range of what people write into their artist statements. Of most importance is that you write something.

If you are exhibiting a well-made functional piece, your intention is clear. Selvedges and beat are even. You've chosen appropriate materials, and the size is what it should be for the intended use. But if you have tried something innovative that the viewer or a judge might not understand, you need to include an artist statement on the entry form or exhibit label. Maybe you prefer wonky selvedges or you've spun milkweed silk into the weft, viewers (and judges) appreciate knowing about how your piece is different.

Figure 7.5 Pam Farley, Sonia. Dupioni silks and cottons, wire, wooden base. 18 x 12 in. Courtesy of artist.

An artist statement becomes even more essential if there is content or a concept, particularly in an abstract piece, such as *Sonia* by Pam Farley (England, 1943), shown in Figure 7.5. Farley says of this three-dimensional piece: "Sonia (meaning wisdom). She was beautiful, bright, and brave and my friend, but her life was too brief." Consider the following questions as you sort out what you might like to communicate to the viewer about your own work:

- Did I start with another weaver's pattern? How did I change it? What was my design influence?
- Did I use unusual materials?
- Did I use an unusual loom or invent tools or a process in order to execute the piece?
- Why was I driven to make it? What was my inspiration?
- What or who has had the greatest influence on my work?
- How is my work different from that of other weavers?
- What do I want people to understand about myweaving? What is the concept?
- Is there something about the piece I want to hold close to my chest, rather than write or talk about it? If so, is there some less private aspect that would help the viewer understand and appreciate my work?

Once you have thought through these questions, you can select those areas that you think would be most helpful to include in an artist statement. How much depends upon the required length. Often it is no more than 50 words that will fit on an exhibit label. However, it might be a full page for your website.

Meeting Seven: Weave Your Passion

As you describe the meaning of your piece in the artist statement, consider allowing the viewer the opportunity to develop their own meaning by being a little ambiguous. You can tease them a little so that every viewer will have their own interpretation. No rules here. It is up to you how specific you want to be.

Some Weavers and their Artist Statements

Each of the following contemporary weavers has a different approach to writing an artist statement. But all of them have been able to articulate meaningfully about their inspiration, concept, or intention. Note that Cynthia Schira writes that she doesn't have a concept within her *Cypher* series. That works fine, since she is showing she understands what an artistic concept is, but rejected its importance in her work. In most cases, the quotes represent only a selected section of a longer artist statement.

Lia Cook "My current practice explores the sensuality of the woven image and the emotional connections to memories of touch and cloth. Working in collaboration with neuroscientists, I am investigating the nature of the emotional response to woven faces by mapping in the brain these responses and using the laboratory experience both with process and tools to stimulate new work in reaction to these investigations."

Figure 7.6 Lia Cook. *Tracks Remind*, 2010. Jacquard woven, cotton, rayon. Courtesy of the artist.

Vicki Essig "I am fascinated with light and translucency, the contrast between the fragile, and the strong. With natural materials, I show the small and delicate as the powerful and significant....(M)y hope is that you will for at least a moment, become lost in the discovery of the minute, the quiet of repetition, and the beauty of nature and pattern."

Figure 7.7 Vicki Essig. *Maple Seeds*, 2011, Handwoven silk, stainless steel, with maple seeds, stitched. Courtesy of the artist.

Erika Lynn Hanson "Using the series of the same name by Hudson River Valley school painter Frederic Church as the impetus, *The Icebergs* is a project investigating the possibilities of representing, reinterpreting, and reenacting the view or experience associated with a landscape."

83

Innovative Weaving

Figure 7.8 Erika Lynne Hanson, *Iceberg* 6 (after Frederic Church) 2011. woven linen, 18" x 20". Courtesy of the artist.

Sheila Hicks "Weavings are as permanent a material as wood or bricks or metal, their only enemy is glue – sometimes used to hold the fibers in place – and direct sunlight... One thing is sure, a fiber artist had better know the difference between ample and heavy – between graceful and hefty." (See Figure 3.4)

Ruth Laskey "It's all based on my thinking about giving the loom its own expression, and thinking about what forms can come out of the patterning. Then thinking about how I can push that in various directions... I'm interested in seeing where it takes me, and following the process along that journey—seeing how far the loom will take me."

Rilla Marshall "Through the craft medium of hand-weaving, my work explores changes to population and place in the Atlantic Canadian provinces. Using statistical and geographical data as my raw source materials, I am interested in the translation of factual information into tangible object by physically linking several spheres of knowledge with warp and weft. In an East Coast culture whose identity is largely shaped by a sense of place, my work charts the lay of the land generated by information about changes to the terrain and to the lives of those who live here. My work relies on the grid of handwoven cloth as an organizational system for communication and as a tool for the re-interpretation of technical data from other fields of study. Hand-weaving is a way of re-claiming this information, making it tangible through the process of weaving itself as well as through the narrative nature of cloth.

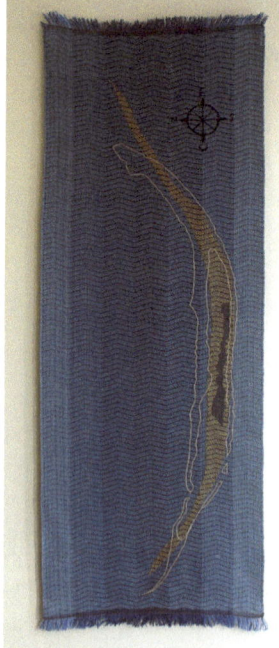

"Incorporating overshot patterning (a traditional form of woven blanket), embroidery and hand-spun wool, I build imagery in cloth that examines the past and the future of our coastal environment. The techniques I am employing to make this work are specific to the weaving and textile heritage of the Atlantic region and explore our cultural legacy of hand-crafted objects of necessity and comfort."

Rowland Ricketts "Today, with petroleum-derived indigo readily and cheaply available, my choice to plant, transplant, weed, harvest, winnow, dry, and compost indigo by hand is not one of necessity. Instead it is a conscious act of recognition that all the energy extended in the farming and processing of the indigo plants is just as much a part of the final dyestuff as the indigo molecules themselves.

Figure 7.9 Rilla Marshall. *Sable Island*, 2011. Handwoven and embroidered, 53 x 23.5 in. Courtesy of the artist.

Meeting Seven: Weave Your Passion

"I find great value in this connection indigo provides to a greater human tradition. Of equal value to me is the time and energy I invest in the farming, processing, and fermenting of this dye. As a dyer I strive to transfigure all the energy of human endeavor expended on this dye so that its vitality lends it life to and lives on in the dyed cloth."

Figure 7.10 Roland Ricketts, III. *Untitled Noren Partition 11*, 2006. Indigo dyed hemp kibra, paste resist, 60 x 60 in. Textile Museum, Washington, DC. Courtesy of the artist.

Jeremy Chase Sanders "Synaesthesia is a neurological phenomenon that causes sense-pairing in the brain. The type of synaesthesia I experience causes me to see a particular color associated with every number and letter of the alphabet (ie '2' is red, 'E' is green). I dye threads to match the colors I see in language and weave cloth with coded text. "I use this process to elucidate the subtle dialogues at work just beneath the surface of the fabrics we use to clothe our bodies and the spaces

Figure 7.11 Jeremy Chase Sanders. *Fabricating Masculinity: Queer Plaids, Gay/Fag, Fairy, Queen, Pansy, Clone*, 2006. Handwoven, hand dyed cotton, 36 x 144 ea. Courtesy of the artist.

85

we inhabit. By imbuing cloth with coded meaning and fashioning it into particular patterns and forms, I examine the words we share and the intricate political hierarchies at play within our language.

"Furthermore, by hand making cloth in a meticulous traditional method I encourage my viewers to question the source of this seemingly ubiquitous material, and the socio-economic issues behind its production."

Cynthia Schira "In these works I focused on the multiple and enticing methods of encryption rather than the content of what was being encrypted. I continue to emphasize the visual and physical rather than the conceptual as I aim for a provocative result."

Figure 7.12 Cynthia Schira. *Small Notes,* Cipher Series, 2007. Cotton, silk, jacquard woven, 29 x 26 in. Courtesy of the artist.

Exercises

These exercises give you an opportunity to consider those issues, things, and people that are most important to you and how you might bring that passion into your weaving. Also, using your Open Creativity, you will practice inventing content and intention for a purely functional scarf. This exercise should prepare you to write an artist statement for your own work.

Exercise 7.1 (30 minutes)

Ten Minutes List those things you most care about. What issues do you find yourself arguing with people about, when you just can't keep your mouth shut? What type of story upsets you most when you see it on tv? What organizations do you belong to that are dedicated to making some sort of change or represent something that is important to you? Are there more personal loves or hates you want to express? After you have your hot points listed, write down possible ways to represent these passions in your weaving.

Twenty Minutes Share two or three of your passions and how you might add that content to your weaving. Feel free to hold back those that you aren't ready to share with the group, but do keep your list for further reference and inspiration.

Exercise 7.2 (30 minutes)

Ten Minutes Write a possible artist statement for the scarf pictured in Figure 7.13. If you find yourself imagining how to modify the piece in order to add content to it, describe that and write the artist statement to reflect the revised piece.

Twenty Minutes Share your artist statement and describe any changes you would make to the design if you were to weave it.

Figure 7.13 Mickey Stam, Scarf, 2011.

Conclusion

This chapter should have given you an opportunity to consider the future direction of your weaving practice. Will you use your Focused Creativity to further develop your craftsmanship and then show your work in environments that most value skill over artistic content? Or will you explore ways to communicate your personal vision through your weaving?

If you decide to seek new opportunities for exhibiting your work, treat any possible rejection as an opportunity to learn about the expectations of the different venues. From there you have a choice to attempt to meet those expectations next time or look for a venue that better fits your current work. Rejection is not a statement that your work is bad, only that it doesn't meet the needs of that gatekeeper.

We hope that some of you are ready to express your passions in new ways through your weaving. And whether through concept art or functional craft, we encourage you to take many opportunities for exhibition so that others can view and appreciate your creative efforts.

Further Sources for Inspiration

Pinterest. Search "conceptual weaving"

Brown Grotta Arts, www.browngrotta.com A gallery that represents fiber artists.

Google all the concept artists mentioned in this chapter.

Innovative Weaving

MEETING EIGHT: FOCUS YOUR WEAVING

In the previous chapter, we downplayed the importance of craftsmanship in our weaving, while we and how developing skills enhances the ability to communicate the desired message. We will highlight how a photograph can provide both inspiration and the materials for a weaver today.

For this study group meeting, **please bring a smartphone or digital camera. Also bring a family or travel photograph that has significance to you.**

A Very Brief History of Photography

While people were experimenting with capturing images with a camera as early as 1800, it wasn't until the Industrial Revolution when the growing middle class created a demand for relatively inexpensive portraits that Louis Daguerre (France, 1787-1851) introduced a practical method for creating a photograph. The daguerreotype, first available in 1839, eventually overcame the oil painting as the preferred method of preserving the family's images.

Figure 8.1 Sisters in Plaid. Ohio, c. 1865.

Technology continued to advance, making it easier for both the professional photographer and the subject, particularly when the length of time someone had to sit without moving was cut from several minutes to a few seconds. However, the daguerreotype was limited to only a single photograph per shot, since the camera produced a positive image directly onto a copper plate with no medium for copying the photograph. By the late 1850's professionals, like Civil War photographer Mathew Brady (American, 1822-1896), were using glass plate negatives that allowed multiple prints to be made. Then in the 1890's photographers began to use the lighter weight and more convenient plastic negative film.

It wasn't until 1901, when George Eastman introduced the Kodak Brownie camera with easily replaceable roll film, that the average consumer had the ability to take their own travel and family black and white photos. In 1936, Kodak introduced color for the mass market in the form of Kodachrome 35mm color slides. Developing the film and producing prints for both black & white and color continued to require darkroom skills to operate the equipment, the lighting, and manage the chemicals.

While anyone might have been able to take a photograph by the beginning of the 20th century, the difference between the amateur's pictures and that of the professional was obvious. Magazines like the weekly *Life* from 1936 until 1972 and the long-lived *National Geographic Magazine* celebrated the photographer's ability to skillfully use lighting, focus, contrast, and composition to tell a story and create an atmosphere. *National Geographic Magazine* was an early adaptor of color, publishing a tinted black and white photo in 1910 and its first color film photograph in 1914. It wasn't until 1962 when it published a complete issue of color images. But good photos required more than a nature scene. In order to spark up an otherwise monotone color photo, such as a green mountain view or a dark interior, the *National Geographic* photographer often added someone or thing in bright red. Imagine how uninteresting the photograph in Figure 8.3 would be without the woodpecker's red head and yellow on her beak. Possibly derisively, this became known as the Red Shirt School of Photography. But the trick is worth considering for your own work.

Figure 8.2 Female Red-bellied Woodpecker.

Professional photographers continued to use cameras with settings that let them control the light, depth of field, and focus, rather than the simpler consumer equipment. They often developed their own film, making necessary adjustments in light, contrast, tint, and composition in the darkroom, in order to ensure their final photographs met their expectations as much as possible.

While photojournalists were tasked with recording what they saw, the Pictorialist style of photography, popular from around 1885 until about 1915, staged scenes and costumed subjects to produce an expressive image similar to that of a painting. They often used a soft focus and occasionally even added visible brush strokes. Alfred Stieglitz (American, 1864-1946), the best-known of the Pictorialists, said:

> Photography is not an art. Neither is painting, nor sculpture, literature or music. They are only different media for the individual to express his aesthetic feelings.

By the late 1920's, West Coast photographers, such as Ansel Adams (1902-1984), Imogen Cunningham (1883-1976), and Edward Weston (1886-1958), were striving for a different aesthetic, one that celebrated sharp focus in both foreground and background. Long exposure was usually required, thus the subject needed to be still or moving very slowly. These men and women wanted their work to be seen as pure photography, with no reference to any previous art form. Seven of them came together in 1932 for a show called "Group f/64" at the M.H. de Young Memorial Museum in San Francisco. Group f/64 was a reference to the small lens aperture opening in a camera, which produces a sharply focused depth of field throughout the image.

In his efforts to improve the quality of black and white photography, Ansel Adams collaborated with the Hollywood portrait photographer Fred R. Archer (American, 1889-1963) around 1939-1940 to develop the Zone System, which provided techniques and calculations for producing the ultimate range of contrast from true black through the entire gray scale to true white within a single photograph. The system helped compensate for the limitations of light meter readings and photosensitive materials.

In 1990, the first digital camera, the Logitech Fotoman, became available. Ten years later a camera was on the Sharp J-Phone. Today most of us have a camera on our smartphones, which automatically makes decisions about the best light and focus settings. In addition, we can instantaneously distribute the images to friends and followers. Meanwhile skilled photographers can still choose to process their own film or go digital and make adjustments using professional-level editing software. Years of experience and training continue to be required to create a well-crafted photograph, and then art only comes with the addition of an aesthetic sensibility.

Meeting Eight: Focus Your Weaving

Applying Camera Controls to Weaving

A camera has many settings to control the quality of the light and focus in the resulting image. The craft of photography is in the ability to use the camera's settings appropriate for different situations and how then to fine tune the captured image in the darkroom or the digital image in photo editing software. With a little stretch of the imagination, each of these adjustments can help you think about how you design and, equally important, how you execute your weaving.

Focus

In order to ensure a sharp image, either the object being photographed or the camera lens may need to be moved. We develop expectations for the amount of sharp edges in a photographic subject depending on the environment. For instance, we tolerate a certain amount of fuzziness of the subject in a newspaper or portrait, less in a fashion magazine, and none in most photographs in a museum. Anything out of this tolerance better have a good reason or we attribute the blurriness to the photographer's lack of skill or the editor or curator's ineptitude.

Figure 8.3 Robin Nest, 2016.

We can apply those expectations for sharp, intentional edges to weaving also. Our eyes quickly pick up threading and treadling errors that mar the pattern. In addition, we usually want to see straight selvedges, otherwise our eye can be distracted from the rest of the work. If the selvedges are uneven, we need to know that it is intentional and not the result of the weaver's lack of control.

Aperture

The aperture setting or f-stop controls the size of the opening to the camera's lens and thus the amount of light passing through. The smaller the size of the opening the more the subject and background are in focus, the larger the size the less is in focus. This is called depth of field. Thus in the large opening of f/2.8 the subject might be in focus, but the foreground and background will likely be fuzzy. The robin eggs in Figure 8.3 were shot in f/4, so you can see that the eggs are in sharp focus while the twigs in the nest closest to the camera are blurred, as is the grass in the background.

In the small opening of f/32 all of a landscape from a nearby tree to a distant mountain will be sharp. But the f/2.8 opening requires much less ambient light for a correct exposure than the f/32. In portrait photography, a relatively large aperture, such as f/5, may be used to emphasis the sitter by intentionally blurring the foreground and background.

As you design a weaving, consider what you want to be in focus and what you want to be as mere background. If everything is in sharp focus, the piece may appear too cluttered. We may use subtler colors or smaller patterns or simply tabby in the background to create more of a blur, thus highlighting other elements. Of most importance, pay attention to what should be merely background and where you want attention focused.

Innovative Weaving

Shutter speed

The adjustment that controls the length of time that the shutter allows light through the lens is its speed. The brighter the available light, the less time required. The lower the light, the more time required. Movement is a factor to consider here. The more movement the more light is required, otherwise the image may blur. Notice the ability of the digital camera on automatic to freeze the motion in Figure 8.4.

Figure 8.4 Cowboy Church Roping Event, Liberty Hill, Texas.

It might be a stretch, but we can consider the motion of throwing the shuttle as a controlled speed also. When all your movements are habitual, you have an even beat with all the wefts equal distance from each other. And when they are not, the uneven beat inevitably calls attention to itself. When we see irregular changes in the number of picks per inch, we usually assume it is happening because the weaver wasn't paying attention to the steady rhythm of his or her movements. Both the correct shutter speed for the amount of movement in a photograph and the steady rhythm of a shuttle through the shed significantly contribute to the quality of the final product.

ISO Speed

Depending upon the expected availability of light, film photographers choose a particular type of film according to its sensitivity to light, which is defined as its ISO (previously ASA) speed. The smaller the ISO number the more light must be available for a correct exposure, such as on a sunny day, and the larger the ISO number the less light available, such as a night. The film camera needs to be adjusted to the film's recommended speed in order for the exposure meter to read accurately. The digital camera also has an ISO speed setting that only needs to be changed when the camera is on manual. The wrong ISO speed setting can leave you with an incorrectly exposed or a grainy image no matter what other adjustments you make.

The ISO speed of the film is similar to the recommended size or yards per pound of the yarn we want to use for a project, such as found in *Handwoven*'s Master Yarn Chart, which shows what sett (ends per inch) to use for specific yarns. You can then chose an appropriate reed and check a reed table to determine how many ends to sley.

Like the light sensitivity of the film, the yarn you choose for a project is also affected by the light that hits it. The color, luster, and texture all determine how light will be reflected. Smooth pearl cotton and reeled silk reflect more light than wool. Is the yarn appropriate for the expected illumination? Should you add a little bit of white or yellow to a pillow that will sit in a dark corner?

White Balance

One sign of a skilled photographer is the ability to produce the whitest white and the blackest black. Large area of dark or light within a shot can cause inaccurate readings from an exposure meter, digital or not, resulting in reduced contrast and whites and/or blacks grayed out. Many approaches have been developed over the years, such as taking the meter reading off of a gray card and making the adjustments in the dark room. Today we can quickly compensate for a digital camera's

Meeting Eight: Focus Your Weaving

incorrect reading by making adjustments in photo editing software, such as Mac Photos, Adobe Photoshop, or Picasa. The photo in Figure 8.5 was taken against a white brick wall. Notice how the reading on the pink wrap caused the wall to also appear pink and the wrap itself dark. By increasing the exposure of the image in Photos until the pink wall appeared white, the silk wrap was returned to its more accurate colors. Notice the scales on the dragon's tail now are white, rather than pink in Figure 8.5.

Figure 8.5 John Marshall, Wrap. Untouched digital photo.

Figure 8.6 John Marshall, Wrap, silk. Digital photo exposure increased in Mac Photo.

While you can use this technique to improve the photographs you take of your work, consider the value of using clear whites and blacks in your weaving to sharpen the effect of a design. It doesn't need to be a lot of either, but black and white can help clarify the other colors in textiles as they do in a photograph.

Composition

While not a setting on a camera, effective composition is as vital to a good photo as its exposure and focus. A common approach to placement of the main subject in a photograph is to divide the image with two equally placed lines vertically and horizontally, creating nine boxes. Usually the center box is avoided, instead the main subject is best placed closer to where the boxes intersect. Is the subject of the photo adequately highlighted? Are distractions cut out of the composition? Is the subject placed pleasantly within the frame?

Figure 8.7 Cotton Gin Ruins, Elgin, TX, 2015

Figure 8.8 Flipped Image, Cotton Gin Ruins, Elgin, TX

Cultural differences show up in how we "read" a photograph. Trained by the way we read Western text, our eyes scan from left to right, thus they prefer pictures that have something on the right to stop our eye movement. Do you have a preference for Figure 8.7 or the flipped version in Figure 8.8?

Fortunately, with today's photo editing software, we can use the cropping tool to punch up a relatively boring or cluttered photo. Figure 8.9 has far too much going on. By using the cropping tool in Mac Photos and increasing the exposure, the yarn and spindle bowls become the point of the image in Figure 8.10.

Innovative Weaving

Figure 8.10 Sarah Monger, Yarn and spindle bowls, tumbler, etc. Cropped image.

Figure 8.9 Sarah Monger, Booth at WEST Studio Tour, Austin, TX, 2015. Full image.

As we compose our weaving design, we need to ask the same questions we do when taking a picture or editing a digital image. Am I highlighting what I want the viewer to look at? Is there something that distracts the eye from what I want the viewer to focus on? Would placing the subject off-center be more interesting?

Most of us would recognize the image in Figure 8.10 as that of an amateur photographer. A professional commercial photographer has the equipment, lighting, camera skills, and experience necessary for the quality images needed for publication or fine craft show entry forms. In photography, as in weaving, skilled workmanship shows through.

Importance of Craftsmanship

Despite all the automatic settings in today's cameras and the ability of us consumers to print our own photographs, the years of training and experience continues to shine through the work of a skilled photographer. Photographers with the craft under their belts have a greater chance of creating beautiful and meaningful images.

Portrait and fashion photographer Annie Liebovitz (American, b. 1949) has made the transition from the darkroom to digital photography, embracing Adobe Photoshop, particularly as it helps her create the conceptual atmospheres that are the signature of her portraits. But the craft is central. She says "Those who want to be serious photographers, you're really going to have to edit your work. You're going to have to understand what you're doing. You're going to have to not just shoot, shoot, shoot. To stop and look at your work is the most important thing you can do." In addition, Liebovitz says that "I fight to take a good photograph every single time."

Beth Moon (American, b. 1956) uses a forty-year old Pentax 6x7 camera, as well as a digital SLR, to take her magnificent photos of the world's oldest trees. She says "I cannot imagine a better way to commemorate the lives of the world's most dramatic trees, many which are in danger of destruction, than by exhibiting their portraits." In addition to the obvious control of her camera, her final images benefit from platinum printing. In a YouTube video of her process, she uses a negative the size of the final image for a contact print and 100% cotton paper to create photographs that are expected to last thousands of years. Moon says:

> In a market that places a high premium on archival work, the struggle increases to balance art, commerce and technique. Crossing the line from machine made to handmade does necessitate a commitment, and true, the work is labor intensive, but the finished results ensure a satisfaction that comes with the freedom to define many decisions while working with materials that allow you to be

Meeting Eight: Focus Your Weaving

true to your vision. And in the end, what unfolds before your eyes is more of an "art-object" than an ordinary photograph.

Such commitment to craft of photography is foreign to most people. All they need today is to take quick, recognizable shots with their ubiquitous smartphones that they can instantaneously send to their friends and followers. The craft is completely irrelevant.

The same might be said about the craft of weaving. Automation now controls the quality of nearly 100% of the knitted and woven fabric used for apparel, household goods, and industrial materials throughout the world. Selvedges are straight, beat is even, threading and treadling errors are rare, and costs are minimized. A modern air-jet machine can lay down 1800 yards of weft per minute. The market seems to believe the cheap costs are worth the sacrifice of uniqueness and often quality.

Yet, here are handweavers acquiring inefficient hand-operated looms, expending time and materials making only one or two items per design and warp, and then trying to sell them for sometimes over 50 times what a similar item would cost at Target. What is it that drives us to what some might consider utter insanity?

Part of the explanation can be found in David Pye's *The Nature and Art of Workmanship* where he writes about the difference between the "workmanship of risk" and the "workmanship of certainty." The latter is demonstrated by industrial looms that are built to tightly control every aspect of the weaving process. Quite different is the setup and operation of our handlooms, which shows the workmanship of risk. At any moment we can make a threading error, break a warp thread, or press the wrong treadle, marring our work. Our experience, training, and minute-to-minute concentration determine our ability to produce a well-made object. Maybe that challenge is what hooks us. It is a never ending struggle, no matter how long we have been weaving, our guard most always be up to demonstrate, mostly to ourselves, that we have the discipline to manage that risk. The longer we weave, the easier it is for our hands to execute some of the process, but the risk is always there that our attention will be drawn away by a phone call or a child, and a mistake maybe the result.

Most of us handweavers become bored by what we have done before. The challenge is behind us, thus we take another class on a new technique or experiment with a complex pattern or different yarn. We are looking for the satisfaction that comes from using our patience to gain some control over a new skill.

Conference and guild classes, with instructors like Laura Fry and Peggy Osterkamp, can help you learn how to dress your loom and control your body movements to get the most consistency in your cloth. While it is fun and informative to take classes, it is coming home and practicing what you have learned over and over again that makes you a productive and skilled weaver.

Certificate programs like the Handweavers Guild of America's Certificate of Excellence in Weaving and the Guild of Canadian Weavers Certification (CWC) program are excellent ways to learn a wide range of weave structures, patterns, and techniques while also practicing methods for producing well-crafted work. Consider that in the CWC exam a whole exercise is disqualified if there is one threading or sleying mistake or two treadling mistakes. The discipline learned in either of these programs can't but help you to improve the quality of your work.

Innovative Weaving

Fine craftsmanship isn't a requirement for artistic expression. However your craftsmanship shouldn't distract from what you are trying to say. Or as David Pye says, "Good workmanship is that which carries out or improves upon the intended design. Bad workmanship is what fails to do so and thwarts the design." He warns that poor execution may thwart the maker's intentions:

> The workman's achievement may differ from the idea for three separate reasons: it may do so because he intends that it shall, it may do so because he has not time to perfect the work, and finally it may do so because he has not enough knowledge, patience or dexterity to perfect it. The last of these reasons is the one with which every layman is familiar, and hence to the layman's rough workmanship often suggests ineptitude.

For many, if not most, of today's handweavers, artistic expression is less important than the satisfaction found in exploring weaving's traditions and continually honing their technical skills. Inga Marie Carmel, a WSSA member, is one of those weavers. Descended from generations of Swedish weavers, her passion is researching and pushing the traditions of her heritage, often through weaving with linen and geometric patterns.

Figure 8.10 Marie Carmel, Dukagang Pillow. *Handwoven*, September/October 2015. Photograph by Joe Coca and courtesy of Interweave. Copyright © Interweave.

Sharine Kirchoff (ryukyuheritagetextiles.com), a member of Contemporary Handweavers of Houston, Texas, also celebrates her heritage through her double ikat dyeing and weaving. The top in Figure 8.11 has been resist dyed in both the warp and the weft, using the traditional Kasuri techniques practiced in Okinawa, Japan. The honoring of these cultural traditions through their skilled and beautiful execution in both Kirchoff and Carmel's work is enough. No deeper concept is needed. They express the pure joy many of us feel about our chosen craft of weaving.

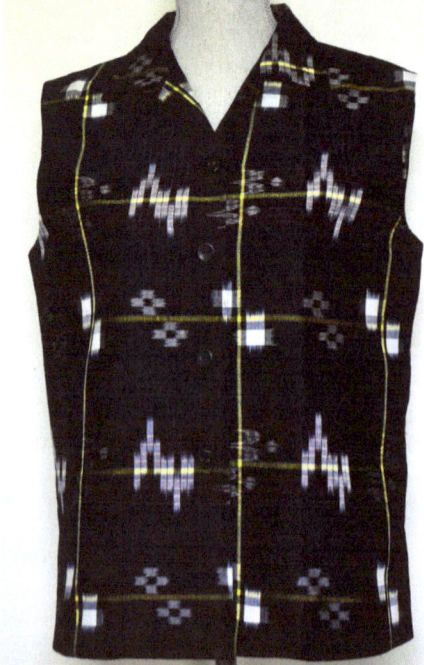

Figure 8.11 Sharine Kirchoff. Kashuri shirt, 2014. Cotton, commercial dyes. Resist-tied and hand-dyed kasuri ikat threads, handwoven, hand-stitched, machine sewn. Courtesy of artist.

Meeting Eight: Focus Your Weaving

Using A Photograph With Your Weaving

The following ideas are only a few of the ways you may use photographs in your weaving.

Cut It Up

You can print a photograph onto paper-backed cotton or silk, cut it into continuous strips, and use them as a weft. You can carefully place the strips in the warp so the image remains recognizable or just lay it in haphazard to get a sense of the image, but use it for texture and color.

Inspire You

Photographs can open you up to new ways of seeing the world, particularly by focusing your attention to patterns you may have not previously noticed. They can remind you of important events in your life or call your attention to colors and patterns that work well together.

Figure 8.12 Eileen Thompson, Shawl.

Figure 8.13 *Morning Light San Miguel*. Photograph by Olof Carmel.

Several years ago, WSSA had a weaving challenge using the photographs of Olof Carmel, the brother of WSSA member Inga Marie Carmel, for inspiration. Guild member Eileen Thompson made a lovely shawl in earth tones that replicated colors and rectangles in Carmel's street scene. (See Figure 8.12 and 8.13.)

As you look through a magazine, pay attention to those photos that grab your attention. What are the colors being used? What is the percentage of each color, including the neutrals? Would these work for a weaving?

Trace It

You can make a pattern from a photograph for tapestry, drawloom, or pickup doubleweave, as Katie Winter did here for a small art quilt. She placed her photo on a light box, followed by tracing paper. She drew out the various elements she was going to applique, and then took the drawing to a copy center to be blown up to the size of the final quilt. The copy was the pattern for her individual applique pieces. Figure 8.15 shows the pattern and Figure 8.16 the final quilt.

Figure 8.14 Original photo, Katie Winter

Innovative Weaving

Figure 8.15 Tracing from photo, Katie Winter. Courtesy of the artist.

The same technique can be used to create a pattern for tapestry and pickup double weave. But instead copy the pattern onto graph paper.

Figure 8.16 Katie Winter, Painted Turtle. Appliqued quilt, cotton. Courtesy of the artist.

Exercises

The following exercises give you an opportunity to use your own photographs for inspiration.

Exercise 8.1 (30 minutes)

Ten Minutes Study a family or travel photo that has particular significance to you. Write down as many ideas that you can on how you might interpret it in a weaving.

Twenty Minutes One at a time, share one or two of your ideas with the group and note any subsequent ideas that come to mind.

Exercise 8.2 (30 minutes)

Fifteen Minutes Using your smartphone or digital camera, walk around your meeting space, including outside, taking pictures of repetitive, interesting patterns.

Fifteen Minutes One at a time, share one or two of your images, describing possible uses in your weaving.

Conclusion

The craft of photography has much to teach us about our weaving. In both expressions, our best work is produced when we learn and respect the traditions of the craft, when we continually practice our skills, and when we pay close attention to our work as we perform it. Through the workmanship of risk, we are able to both celebrate weaving's traditions and express our individual vision.

Further Resources for Inspiration and the Study of Our Craft

Google the following masterful photographers: Ansel Adams, Annie Leibovitz, Gordon Parks, and Edward Weston

Meeting Eight: Focus Your Weaving

Moon, Beth. *Ancient Trees: Portraits of Time*. Abbeville Press, 2014.

Osterkamp, Peggy. All of her weaving guides.

Salt of the Earth. Documentary about Sebastião Salgado, a Brazilian photographer. Incredible work with composition and texture, all in black and white.

Weaving classes, such as at:

- Penland School of Craft, Spruce Pine, North Carolina
- Joseph C. Campbell Folk School, Brasstown, North Carolina
- Arrowmont School of Arts and Crafts, Gatlinburg, Tennessee
- Sätergläntan Institute of Crafts, Sweden
- Västuga Weaving School, Shelburne, MA
- Handweavers Guild of America's biennial Convergence Conference
- Regional conferences
- Of course, guild classes

Innovative Weaving

MEETING NINE: FASHION YOURSELF A COLLECTION

Well-known artists, including fashion designers, have mastered the ability to develop a cohesive series or collection of their work. Each series has a overarching theme that ties the pieces together. The collection furthers the public's understanding of the artistic intention of the creator. Many of you work this way already, but others find your head turned by the latest weaving class, book, or magazine. Your body of work is thus comprised of many different structures, patterns, styles, and materials. Nothing connects them other than you as the weaver. This exploration can be a valuable exercise, particularly for a new weaver, but this chapter helps you consider the advantages of intentionally building on your work into recognizable series.

We will define the different fashion categories, such as haute couture, and how they might help you look at your own work in a new light. We also encourage you to seek inspiration from the textile innovations as they appear on high-end runway shows.

A Very Brief History of Fashion Collections

Selecting a ready-made dress from variations within a collection wasn't possible for women until the mid-19th Century. Men's suits became available off-the-rack after the War of 1812, but women continued to wear clothing made specifically to their measurements and tastes by themselves, family members, or dressmakers.

Figure 9.1 Sears, Roebuck Catalog, 1902.

The big change for women's fashion occurred in 1858, when Charles Frederick Worth (English, 1825-1895) opened the House of Worth in Paris. Worth presented himself, not as a dressmaker, but as a designer or couturier, telling women what they should wear as defined by two seasonal collections a year.

His innovations included presenting his designs on live models and sewing his branded label into his garments. Worth eliminated the popular large round crinoline by creating a more practical flatter silhouette in the front and sides, with a bustle in the back. As the first haute couture designer, Worth's greatest legacy may be his elevation of apparel designers to the influential status they continue to have today.

While women with significant means might select their wardrobe from a Worth couture collection, the upper middle class might have a French design copied by a dressmaker. Sears, Roebuck and Co. begun as a mail order company in 1886, provided an alternative for many women of lesser means and in rural areas. You could buy women's capes and undergarments in limited sizes from Sears, but dresses and suits were still not "off the rack." However for a dress or suit in 1902, you selected a design and then mailed in your bust size and length measurement. Apparently you were on your own to alter the garment's waist and hips.

101

Innovative Weaving

Within twenty years, women's ready-to-wear in set sizes became available as seen in the 1922 Sears, Roebuck catalog. (Figure 9.2) In the same year, Mary Schenck Woolman published a comparison of clothing costs that may reveal the inferior quality of the $5.98 blue wool "French serge" dress in the 1922 Sears catalog, on the left in Figure 9.2. Woolman found the following average costs for making a wool dress:

Made at home $16.25
Ready-to-wear $25.00
Dressmaker $30.90

Consider these costs when the average clothing expenditures for a "self-supporting" woman were around $125 per year. Today we may complain that it is more expensive to make a garment at home than it is to buy it at Target. When you compare the $5.98 Sears dress to Woolman's $16.25 made-at-home dress it appears that the cost disparity has been around since manufactured ready-to-wear clothing. It appears it has long been more expensive to make quality apparel at home than it is to buy cheaply made garments off the rack.

Figure 9.2 Sears, Roebuck Catalog, 1922.

A major shift in fashion evolved in the 1940's, first represented by the informal designs of Clair McCardell (American, 1905-1958). In 1934, She developed five pieces of black wool knit that could be configured in different ways to wear for the beach, dinner, and dancing. Her early 1940's collections stressed cotton and comfort, using rectangles and triangles, rather than the structured garments favored in Paris. In the early 1940's she used leotards and black turtleneck sweaters in some of her designs, which foretold the beatnik uniform of the 1950's and early 1960's.

Haute couture houses in Paris continued to present their collections only to private clients until 1948, when Christian Dior shook things up by presenting a line of less expensive versions of his designs at lower prices for the youthful market. Other houses followed, seeing the advantage of incorporating ready-to-wear collections into their lines.

A lesser-known designer, but an influential one, is Georgio di Sant'Angelo (Italian, 1933-1989) who is credited with partnering with manufacturers, like DuPont, to develop innovative knits using synthetic yarns. Before the 1960's and Sant'Angelo's experimentation, most stretch fabrics were made only of wool and cotton. He abhorred buttons and zippers, thus his garments usually slipped over the head and clung to the body without structured layers underneath. It is difficult to imagine fashion today without knit fabrics in their many forms and materials.

Another innovator, but one who works more with wovens, is Issey Miyake (Japanese, b. 1938). He manipulates fabric in new ways, such as pleating to create garments that collapsed and expanded in overall pleating. He also uses many natural colors and handwoven fabrics. He says he finds weaver's mistakes inspiring.

His construction techniques appear to be based on origami, starting off with rectangles and seemingly simple folding for features like lapels. His 1981 Plantation line included an unbleached cotton shirt, which shows his interest in asymmetry and minimalism. Miyaki often works within the Japanese aesthetic called wabi-sabi, which values asymmetry, irregularities, simplicity, and a deep appreciation of natural objects and processes. This influence can be seen in many of the designs for handwovens being made today.

The innovations of Alexander McQueen's (English, 1969-2010) might be considered the antithesis of Miyaki. His tailoring was considered immaculate and his runway shows were known to be shocking fantasies. He only worked within the exclusive club of haute couture beginning in 1996 when he was chief designer for Givenchy. He left Givenchy in 2001 to establish his own fashion house, feeling constrained by the expectations of the brand. After McQueen's years with Givenchy and under his own brand, his collections are considered particularly important because he was able to maintain couture-quality craftsmanship while pushing fashion forward with his edginess.

In this quite selective history of fashion collections, we have covered innovations in lifestyle, in materials, in cultural aesthetics, and in the ability to shock while maintaining exquisite craftsmanship. Another innovation occurred in 2001, when Stella McCartney (English, b. 1971) opened her fashion house. From its inception, she has taken a different approach, focusing on the production processes as much as her designs. Reflecting the values of her parents, Paul and Linda McCartney, her brand and individual collections are based on her commitment to vegetarianism and the ethical treatment of animals. She does not use any leather, fur, or other animal skins, including in her shoe designs. While she may employ fabrics derived from animals, such as wool and silk, she monitors the collection processes, and in 2015 publicly ended a relationship with an Argentinian wool supplier for mistreatment of its sheep.

Edun, founded in 2005 by lead singer and political activist Bono and his wife, Ali Hewson, is another example of a fashion company with an overarching social mission. Edun was started to develop fair-trade relationships with African producers. However, like many other celebrity-led fashion houses, it is dependent upon hired designers. Since 2013, Danielle Sherman has been the creative director, thus the head designer. Process problems in Africa, such as poor quality and delivery slippages, forced them to move the fashion line to China. However they continue to grow the cotton and make their t-shirts in Africa, which comprises 85% of Edun's business. Both McCartney and Edun's experiences only hint at the challenges of the fashion business. Success depends not only on an innovative design collection, but effective forms of promotion, production, and delivery.

You are encouraged to explore the history of fashion and its many designers. Their creativity and enthusiasm for textiles can't help but inspire you and their challenges inform your own business choices. The Further Sources for Inspiration at the end of this chapter provides some websites and books to get you started.

Understanding Fashion Terminology

Unlike the other art forms we have explored, weaving, along with knitting and felting, provides the basic material for all fashion. Well, at least until 3-D printing becomes more economical. Over the last century and a half, eight different terms have developed to describe different approaches to forming that material into clothing. Each provides an opportunity for you to consider how your work might be valued in the marketplace.

Haute-Couture

The term "haute couture" can only be legally used to describe members of Le Chambre Syndicale de las Haute Couture (Trade Union of Parisian High Fashion). In order to be included, a fashion house must meet the following requirements first established in 1945:

Innovative Weaving

- Made-to-order for private clients with one or more fittings
- An atelier (workshop) in Paris with at least 20 full-time employees
- Presentation of two collections a year to the press, with at least 25 runs (outfits), including both daytime and evening wear.

Some of these requirements for specific numbers have been relaxed over the years, but otherwise remain the same. When the syndicate first was formed in 1868, the intention was to prevent people from counterfeiting their designs. The twelve members as of 2015 included Chanel, Christian Dior, Givenchy, and Jean Paul Gaultier. Foreign houses, called correspondent members, include Versace and Giorgio Armani.

When you buy from one of these fashion houses, you are paying for the couturier's unique vision, along with the best fabrics, embellishments, and the skills of the best beaders, embroiderers, and other handcrafters. And, of course, you are also paying for a garment that fits you perfectly. A haute couture garment requires as much as 700 hours to complete, with a minimum of 20 people working on it, thus a daywear piece might cost $12,000. Today the fashion houses make little profit from their haute couture collections. Rather than the European aristocracy that once patronized the fashion houses, clients are mostly coming from the well-heeled of Russia, China, and the Middle East. Some of the few remaining haute couture houses consider their exclusive runway collections merely as glamorous publicity for the brand's other money-making efforts, such as ready-to-wear, perfume, and cosmetics.

Prêt-à-porter (Ready-to-wear)

Ready-to-wear (RTW) or the French term prêt-à-porter refers to apparel that has been manufactured in standard sizes and sold off-the-rack in stores and online. The high-end fashion houses present their RTW collections on the Paris runway in February each year for the Fall/Winter season and in September for Spring/Summer. Dior and Chanel all have RTW collections, at obviously lower price points than their haute couture garments. These collections often carry over ideas explored in a fashion house's haute couture runway show, but without the hand-worked detail and expensive materials. Other designers, such as Stella McCartney and Issey Miyake, also present their collections at these Paris RTW shows. Most Americans, like Ralph Lauren and Proenza Schouler, participate in New York's Fashion Weeks instead. Due to the internet, RTW runway shows are appearing not just in the fashion capitals of Paris, New York, and Milan, but all around the world with images available almost instantly.

Mass Market

The vast majority of our clothing fits within the Mass Market category, which is manufactured within the company's own standardized measurements, is dependent upon designs copied from other collections, cheap materials, and efficient production and delivery processes. Companies, such as H&M and the Gap, sell their clothing in their own stores to customers seeking lower prices. While occasionally a mass market company may attach a celebrity name to a collection, generally these consumers are uninterested in who designed their clothing.

Subjectively speaking, this is a category you don't want to emulate. Why spend all your time and money weaving a dress that can be bought for $15 at Target? The construction techniques and even the designs may be interesting, but if you want to sell your work, it's best to keep your eye on innovative designers using high quality materials and craftsmanship for inspiration.

Meeting Nine: Fashion Yourself a Collection

Handmade

While not as sexy as the term "wearable art," this is a more accurate term for what most garments handweavers produce to sell off-the-rack and for ourselves. The designer is usually the producer, who is focused more on quality than quantity. We sometimes sell at craft shows, small boutiques, and Etsy.com, often struggling with the right price point to cover our costs and make any profit.

Garments in this category are not necessarily one of a kind. Some designers make multiple copies of a design in different colors and sizes, and even hire help with production, rather than make everything themselves.

Most designers of handmade woven apparel strive for a timeless style outside of the fashion trends shown at Fashion Week. In fact, many of the pieces in the biennial Handweavers Guild of America's Convergence Fashion Show are quite similar to patterns for handwovens developed over 30 years ago. These designs are often based on rectangles in order to minimize sewing of seams and any wastage of the yardage.

Figure 9.3 Susan Bussard, Saori Top, 2015.

Saori-style apparel is a more contemporary approach to working with all or most of the handwoven fabric. All about self-expression, eliminating the technical aspects of weaving and sewing, and embracing mistakes. "Weave, Revive, Reflect" results in individualized, intriguing pieces, based on the Japanese aesthetic of wabi-sabi, such as the top by the WSSA member Susan Bussard in Figure 9.3.

Tailoring

Tailors make each design from scratch specifically for the customer measurements, harking back to the dressmakers before 1858. There is no collection or fashion show. Several fittings are required, and the garments are made by hand. "Bespoke" is the term used by the tailors on London's Savile Row for this approach. Highly skilled techniques are necessary for constructing well-made suits, coats, and trousers using quality wool, linen, and silk. A wool overcoat might cost $6,000 on Savile Row. On the other hand, travelers to Vietnam can now have a tailored suit or a copy of a runway dress fitted to their measurements for around $200. Of course, there is the airfare. But you might want to think twice before considering tailoring as a viable way to sell your handwovens, considering the difficulty finding customers willing to pay a reasonable price for the number of hours required for the designing, weaving, and construction.

Made to Measure

Made-to-measure clothing is based on a standard garment pattern, with adjustments for specific measurements, such as bust and waist, like we saw in the 1902 Sears catalog. The garments are then usually factory assembled. A modern example is the Levi Strauss & Co store in New York City's Meatpacking District where you can chose the thread color, type of denim, and style of grommets for your custom fitted jeans, priced from $450-$750.

Wearable Art

Weavers may throw around the term "Wearable Art" a little too loosely. Wearable art is best defined as having an artistic concept behind it and being one of a kind. Those that are known for

Innovative Weaving

specializing in wearable art usually work within a series with an overarching idea. If you Google "Weird World of Groundbreaking Fashion," you will see amazing examples of wearable art in Gabriela Barcenas' blog. Another source for inspiration is the Fashion Clash Festival website that highlights emerging designers.

Costume

A garment made for a particular occasion, such as a theatrical event, is considered a costume. The term is also used for the garments specific to a particular culture or historical period. Costume roleplaying, popularly called cosplay, is an increasingly popular form of performance art, demonstrated by a section of Jo-Ann Fabric store now dedicated to cosplay fabrics, including gold latex and all sorts of sparkles. In Figure 9.4, Shawn Faus and her daughter, Isabella, are dressed as Professor Chaos and Princess Kenny from the television show *South Park* at the RTX gaming and internet conference in Austin, TX in 2016.

While costumes can be bought or rented, many cosplayers enjoy the making of their costumes as much as the actual roleplaying. Skills in sculpture, dressmaking, fiberglass, woodworking, and makeup can all come to play in creating a complex costume. However, as much creative fun can be found in the use of cardboard, aluminum foil, Sculpey, and altered thrift store findings to create characters like Professor Chaos and Princess Kenny.

Figure 9.4 Shawn and Isabella Faus as Professor Chaos and Princess Kenny. RTX, Austin, TX, 2016.

Finding the Theme for a Collection

Whether haute couture or prêt-à-porter, a runway show must have a theme that defines the presented collection and ties all of the pieces together in some way. Established fashion houses have extensive inspiration resources, such as expensive services that project future trends in color, lifestyle, technology, etc. They usually have extensive libraries of past collections that provide ideas for new designs, while helping to maintain continuity within their brand. The designer's team also attends fabric fairs, like Pitti Filati in Florence, Italy, every January and June to see what new yarns and yardage the industry has available. At these shows the designers and their team not only see color and new technology in yarns and knitted goods, but they are introduced to experimental clothing designs and trend inspiration, such as the following theme called Misericordia (Misery):

> A spirit of sacrifice and understatement. Love thy neighbor. In a range of blues that includes a mystical winter sky and volunteers' uniforms. Perfect for

Figure 9.5 Pitti Filati, Florence, Italy, June 2013.

Meeting Nine: Fashion Yourself a Collection

"poor" and ethnic fashions. Fashion that serves a social purpose. That has a content, that conveys a message: the theme rejects opulence and gets down to the bone. A Franciscan spirit of subtraction. The key is making do with little and transforming the simplest things into extraordinary items. In spite of the used and chewed look, the material is precious and luxurious—high-end. The new missionaries of fashion wear worn and tattered Franciscan habits, but the material is noble and spiritual. The cross is a recurring motif in the stitches, in the patterns, in the embroideries, in the prints and in the geometric structure of the garments. A new, contemporary mysticism will inflame fashion. Fashion that looks poor and simple, ethical fashion that becomes more beautiful the older it gets. Knits have mixed textures: mats, baskets, sacks, meshes, the look of the old hand loom and handcrafting. The layers overlap to create body and warmth. Lots of attention to treatments and wash finishes that create a patina of time, And, in the sportswear theme, the same structures are padded and treated with special coatings and resins.

Figure 9.6 Example of "Misericordia." Pitti Filati, Florence, Italy. June 2013.

A designer will react to a projected trend in an upcoming collection by revising the idea to fit within his/her established brand and the expectations of the customers. There can also be a brand series that appears in every collection, including both haute couture and ready-to-wear, such as the Chanel tweed jacket. Coco Chanel designed the first version in 1954. Subsequent versions continue to have most of the same characteristics: no interfacing, four working pockets, logo buttons, braid around the edges, and a chain on the hem to control the drape.

While Chanel used a Scottish factory to weave the tweeds for her jacket, the yardage is now woven at the Paris House of Lesage, which began a weaving workshop in 1995. The yardage can have as many as twelve different yarns in the warp. Karl Lagerfeld (Germany, b. 1933), now Chanel's head designer, continues to update the basic jacket in his Chanel runway shows, playing with collars, trims, and even shapes, so that they fit within the theme of the season's collection. Go to Style.com to see Chanel's latest version.

As Steven Faerm wrote in his *Fashion Design Course,* fashion themes should "innovate and recontexturalize" one or more of the following:

- New technologies
- Interpretations
- Sustainable methods
- Purpose
- Creating new consumer groups

The theme doesn't have to be a short catch phrase, but it needs to be an overarching idea like these for the Spring/Summer 2014 collections:

- Charles Harbison "American luxury in mid-20th Century Caribbean: a visual marriage of contrasts"
- Katherine Polk's for Houghton collection "This season, I was inspired by the simple basket weave on chaise lounges while I was in Miami sitting on the beach."
- Victoria Bartlett for VPL "Leaves a footprint of sweat from acceleration, sustenance, and endurance"

107

Innovative Weaving

For his Spring/Summer 2007 runway show called "Sarabande," Alexander McQueen elaborated, "Things rot. It was all about decay. I used flowers because they die." Early in the life of these collections themes are presented on mood boards and inspiration books to help shape the individual pieces. We will explore this technique for building a series later in the exercises at the end of the chapter.

Study the Runway Shows

We all now have the advantage of seeing every garment shown in the haute couture and RTW fashion shows all over the world via Style.com and similar websites. There is much to learn as you flip through each image. Some sites allow you to zoom in to see details. Of course, there are trends to inspire us, but more importantly, as you look at each model, pay attention to the following:

- What garments are woven, rather than knitted?
- What woven patterns seem to work well?
- What is the scale of the patterning in plaids, etc.?
- How does the fabric drape?
- What shapes did the designer use for woven fabric?
- What garments are in a weight that you would like to work in?
- Is there surface design, such as embroidery or overdyeing, that might liven up your yardage?
- What is the complexity of the woven garment? Is it within your sewing skills?
- How much piecing is done? Or are there only a few cuts into the fabric?
- Can you imagine a way to make the design your own?
- Are you seeing a trend that will be gone in a year or two? Are you looking for a more timeless look?
- What is the theme and how is that varied throughout the collection?
- Are there color, theme, or texture trends that you might want to work into your designs?

Whatever you weave, you will likely find inspiration from the innovations shown during every Fashion Week.

Weaving What You See

As long as you don't attempt to counterfeit a designer's label and sell imitations of a designer's work, you needn't worry about being sued for reproducing a runway garment. Mass market producers do it all the time, making relatively minor changes. And attempting to copy a design you love is an excellent method for learning and working through construction techniques. However, before you start on your own yardage, you will likely want to make the garment first in a commercial yardage of a similar weight to what you want to weave. This will also help you confirm the amount of warp and weft required. Needless to say, you should also sample your fabric and put it through the expected cleaning method before you weave yards of it.

Construction techniques used in couture fashion house are available in books, such as *Couture Sewing Techniques* by Claire B. Shaeffer. Yes, these methods can be rather time consuming, but if you like sewing, these are just new skills to add to your toolbox.

Meeting Nine: Fashion Yourself a Collection

Certainly making a garment out of a rectangle, such as a ruana, is available to those of you uninteresting in sewing more complicated clothing. On the other hand, Daryl Lancaster has been a major influence on contemporary handweavers, encouraging us to cut into our yardage in order to create shaped garments.

Lancaster teaches classes on how to sew a jacket with handwovens, providing many techniques for dealing with seams, buttonholes, finishing, and stabilizing the yardage. She now has a five-part on-demand seminar called *Garment Construction* for handweavers through Interweavestore.com.

Also take the opportunity to sign up for one of the sessions after the HGA Convergence Fashion Show when the judge takes you around the exhibit providing commentary on what works and what doesn't, pointing out details that take away from the success of the handwoven yardage and which ones complement it. The session can only help you improve your own work and its chance to get into the next juried competition.

Figure 9.7 Daryl Lancaster. *LA Attitude*, 2012. Plain weave with supplemental ribbons. Original design. Courtesy of the artist.

Weaving within a Series

Understandably, not all of you are going to be weaving apparel, accessories, home décor, or concept art to sell, thus there is less motivation to develop an overarching theme for a series of your works. However you might find satisfaction in exploring a unifying theme, concept, subject matter, or philosophy to a greater depth than you can in one piece. Consider these advantages of a cohesive series:

- Ability to explore a theme or concept in deeper and deeper ways
- Build on your knowledge and skill
- Save time by building on a newly learned technique, process, or skill
- Become expert on the technique, skill, idea
- Consistent point of view
- Create more nuance within one piece, because of the support of the other pieces
- Idea becomes stronger as it is repeated in different ways

If you are planning to sell or merely exhibit your work, further advantages of a series are:

- Viewers feel they are on a journey with you
- Creates a sense of unity or a body of work
- Demonstrates that you know what you are doing, where you are going, and what you have to do to get there.

One of our study group members Pam James is committed to using yarns she has unraveled from thrift store sweaters and other recycled materials. She started making clutches and shoulder bags using plastic VCR tape in the weft, selling them at a boutique and guild shows. As she made each one, the concept evolved. She tried different handles and straps. Her latest version uses a variable

Innovative Weaving

reed for her rigid heddle loom so that she can incorporate coated wire and a novelty yard, along with vcr tape.

Making twenty-five purses allowed James to build on what she learned about the advantages and problems with the materials. Each one is different, yet they are all clearly a series and are recognizable as her unique work.

Working in a series doesn't mean putting yourself in an uncomfortable box. You can work on more than one series. And if you find yourself feeling too restricted, certainly "go with your bliss." On the other hand, your strength as a weaver likely comes when you find something that excites you and drives you to delve deeper and deeper into it. And when you have an opportunity to exhibit your work, it will seem more powerful when people can see your growth and exploration through a cohesive series.

Figure 9.8 Pamela James, VCR Tape Purse

Inspiration Notebook

One of the more important aspects of developing a fashion house's seasonal collection is to create what is commonly called that season's mood board, which is a source of inspiration and helps create continuity for the garments to be created. This is a distillation of what has been developing as the designer and the team have been researching the next collection. Your *Innovative Weaving* Inspiration Notebook serves the same purpose. In this chapter's exercises, you will start the research for developing a series of weavings based on a theme. It doesn't need to be for apparel or accessories. This is merely an exercise in expanding upon what you already like to weave or what you would like as your next adventure.

Use your notebook as a repository for images of nature, artwork, interiors, architecture, textures, colors, ideas, subjects, anything that intrigues and excites you. Flip through fashion, lifestyle, decorating, gardening, architecture, and nature magazines, tearing out pictures that might contribute to a series theme. Glue them into your notebook, notating what it was that grabbed you, since it is easy to forget later on. At this point, be open, rather than too selective and judgmental. Some of the things to look for as inspiration for a series are:

- A lifestyle your series should fit into
- Your ideal customer (or giftee)
- General mood you want to create
- Colors and combinations you might use
- Shapes you might want to use
- Details you like
- Overall theme or subject that could hold your interest over several pieces
- Textures you like, along with effective textural contrasts

You will begin working on your series ideas in Exercise 9.1 below.

Exercises

The exercises will start you thinking about developing a series of works that will help your customers identify your work and better understand your growth as an artist. Even if you don't sell your work, expanding on one concept saves time researching and learning new skills, yet provides a rich path for exploration.

Exercise 9.1 (30 minutes)

Ten Minutes Flip through a fashion, gardening, or home décor magazine, tearing out pictures that you can add to your Inspiration Notebook for a series you might like to weave. Don't be stuck on one idea, let your eye be open to whatever attracts you. Write on each one what grabs you, such as the color, the texture, the subject, etc. Refer to the bulleted list in the Inspiration Notebook section.

Twenty Minutes One at a time, share two or three of your images and what attracted you.

Exercise 9.2 (30 minutes)

Ten Minutes Review the images you clipped out in Exercise 9.1 and select those that might lead to a series of weavings. Write down the over-arching theme, subject, or concept. Write down some of the possibilities for different pieces that are somehow related to this theme.
Twenty Minutes One at a time, share your series theme and some of the ideas for individual weavings related to the theme.

Conclusion

Whether you weave for clothing and accessories, like scarves and shawls, interior décor, or concept art, the processes fashion houses use to develop a collection have much to teach you. Individual garments on the runway can be inspirational, but the concept of a collection based on a particular theme demonstrates how a cohesive series can strengthen each individual piece and help develop a meaningful body of work.

This approach is not a requirement, only a choice. If you most enjoy continually learning new and diverse techniques and experimenting with them, you should continue on that course. On the other hand, consider that working in a series provides you a depth of understanding and in many cases an economy of materials and time that isn't available when you move from one idea to another with each warp.

Further Sources for Inspiration

Fasanella, Kathleen. *The Entrepreneur's Guide to Sewn Product Manufacturing.* El Paso, Texas: Apparel Technical Svcs, 1998.

FashionClash.nl Festivals for emerging designers

Lancaster, Daryl. "Sewing with Handwoven Fabrics." *Threads,* October/November 2012.

Net-a-porter.com

Noonan, Meg Lukens. *The Coat Route: Craft, luxury and obsession on the trail of a $50,000 coat.* New York, Spiegel & Grau, 2013.

Promostyl.com/blog/en/home Trend agency, but the website provides free trending ideas, without analysis. English language button on upper right side of webpage.

Innovative Weaving

Shaeffer, Claire B. *Couture Sewing Techniques*. Revised and updated. Newtown, CT: Taunton Press, 2011.

Vogue.com Includes all the pieces in all the runway shows.

Whereiseefashion.tumblr.com Very cool site that pairs runway outfits with art and other images.

Also web search all the concept weavers in the section on Artist Statements in Meeting Seven: Weaving your Passion. Each of these artists has posted more than one of their series.

MEETING TEN: WEAVING FOR THE PUBLIC

Educating the public about handweaving in order to keep this ancient craft alive is likely one of your guild's missions, as well as recruiting new members. Demonstrations around town are a common and fun activity that supports that mission. However, there may also be an opportunity to install a more permanent art piece somewhere in your community that many people will see on a daily basis reminding them of weaving, weavers, and your guild.

This chapter explores those big projects that require fundraising and the collaboration of many people, including property owners and city agencies. For many artists, the monumental challenges and the perseverance required to bring a public piece to fruition is a part of the art.

As you read the chapter, consider how you might bring some of that determination into your own work. How might you work around obstacles, both small and large, and push through to experience the satisfaction of completion. In addition, consider how your guild might benefit from working on a public art project and grow as a more cohesive group through the challenges of such an effort.

A Very Brief History of Public Art

Public art is defined as art that is intended to occur in the public domain, outside and freely assessable to all. It is created for a specific site and involves the community and owners of the property. Memorials, such as generals on horses and the Vietnam Veterans Memorial by Maya Lin (American, b. 1959), represent the oldest form of officially sanctioned public art.

Federal support of art beyond memorials expanded when FDR's New Deal created a program called Art in Architecture. One half of one percent of the total construction costs for all government buildings was set aside to purchase contemporary American art for each structure. The concept today continues in programs such as Art in Public Places in cities around the country.

By the 1960s, along with all the other challenges to the status quo, some artists decided to take their art outside, even into the desert, out of the control of agency funders, museum curators, and gallery owners. Their work questioned the academic definition of sculpture, but also defied the commercialization of art, allowing their work to be experienced freely by the public. These "environmental" artists began to make statements about the destruction of the earth's ecological systems and then expanded their work into the urban landscape. Thanks to the creative energy of the artistic rebels and public art initiatives around the country, our communities are exposed to more free art than every before.

Some Types of Public Art

Public art is expressed in many forms today. The following projects and artists represent not only large art intended to be installed outside for everyone to see, but also provide examples of the importance of perseverance to bring these large projects to completion. Public art isn't easy. Roadblocks are inevitable, but these artists, using a half a dozen different forms of public art, were able to work around the obstacles.

Innovative Weaving

Murals

Murals painted by members of a community have become a valuable expression of a local subculture, particularly for those who feel overrun by gentrification and commercialization. Such is the case of the Mexican-American community in East Austin. *La Lotería*, first painted in 1989 on the wall facing a 7-11 convenience store, represented the cards in a popular Mexican game of chance similar to bingo.

Figure 10.1 La Loteria, 1619 E Cesar Chavez St., Austin, TX. 2015.

In the spring of 2015, the mural was painted over during the SXSW Music Festival as part of an art competition. The Chicano community complained to the festival people, who then apologized and donated $13,000 for restoration of the mural. Nine Austin artists, including four of the original artists and six Austin-area high school students, repainted the mural six days a week during the heat of July 2015 and participated in a festive blessing at its completion. *La Lotería* mural demonstrates the strong connection a community can feel toward a work of art.

Another mural in Austin, although this one is ceramic, provides an example of a project involving school children. It is also an example of the challenges involved in a large collaborative community project. The idea of such a project came to Wanda Montemayor as part of an art therapy thesis in 2006. Five years later, in 2011, the 1,200 square foot ceramic mural was dedicated. The mural tells the story of the Deep Eddy swimming pool from the area's early use by Native Americans.

Students from nine Austin schools were involved in making the individual tiles. She drew out the overall life-size design on paper and cut it up to distribute sections to the different teachers to work on. Montemayor finds that students are more connected to their school and community when they create art and are able to see the results everyday.

Figure 10.2 Detail of Deep Eddy Mural, Austin, TX, 2011.

Montemayor and the ceramist Lisa Orr expected the installation to take only a few days. Instead it took over six weeks in the hottest part of a Texas summer. Making all the sections into a cohesive mural turned out to be more challenging than expected, thus additional ceramists were brought in to improve the transitions from one section to another. The final mural is a tribute to Montemayor's vision and her perseverance working with many teachers, craftspeople, and the sponsors, the City of Austin's Art in Public Places and Friends of Deep Eddy.

Meeting Ten: Weaving for the Public

Land and Environmental Art

Public art that is created in nature, using natural materials, is considered Land Art. These works are often ephemeral, existing now only through photographs and recordings. Environmental Art is a more open term, not restricted by the materials, but it often makes a statement about man's effects upon the environment.

Figure 10.3 Andy Goldsworthy, *Storm King Wall*, 1997-1998. Fieldstone, 60" x 2, 278'6" x 32", Storm King Art Center, New York. Photo by bobistraveling, used under CC BY 2.0.

The work of Andy Goldsworthy (British, b, 1956) provides a perfect example of land art. Photography played a major role in his early work, since it was often ephemeral, made of natural materials, such as flower petals, icicles, leaves, twigs, and thorns, in their natural environment. He says "Each work grows, stays, decays—integral parts of a cycle which the photograph shows at its heights, marking the moment when the work is most alive. There is an intensity about a work at its peak that I hope is expressed in the image. Process and decay are implicit."

A 2004 documentary, *Rivers and Tides*, about Goldsworthy and his creative process shows the steady patience required to execute his assemblages. The camera captures his repeated attempts to balance thorns one on another without any adhesive as he struggles with the effects of gravity. His acceptance of the unpredictability and ephemeral nature of his work can be an inspiration for those of us that work with fiber.

Goldsworthy's wall at Storm King Art Center (Figure 10.3) illustrates his more permanent work. Here the wall seems to enter the pond and then continues up a hill on the other side.

Christo (Bulgaria, b. 1935) and Jeanne-Claude (Morocco, 1935-2009) may be the most well-known of the land artists. The married couple has used fabric in all of their work to wrap buildings and bridges and to drape the landscape with poles, cables, and umbrellas for support. They most often use a woven man-made fiber, such as polypropylene and nylon, that is light weight and moves in the breeze.

Figure 10.4 Christo and Jeanne-Claude. *The Gates*. Central Park, New York City, 1979-2005. Photography by Chad Fennell, used under CC BY 2.0.

Christo and Jeanne-Claude embrace the challenging process required to complete their monumental projects, considering the time spent and the roadblocks as part of their art. Gaining approval of the community, such as the 452 landowners in a Japanese valley for *The Umbrellas* in 1991, searching for the perfect site, and finding the necessary funds is an essential aspect of their art. Many years often pass from the time of the first proposal until a project is completed, such as *The Gates* in Central Park (Figure 10.4),

Innovative Weaving

where the first proposal was submitted to the City of New York in 1979 and installation didn't occur until 2005, twenty-six years later.

Christo insists on paying for all of his work with his own money, usually through sale of his designs on paper and his early paintings. He pays for all labor, rather than depending upon volunteers. Installation and security people receive union wages, when appropriate, and minimum wage for the rest.

Despite the effort put into each project, all of Christo's work is intended to be temporary, usually up no longer than a couple of weeks. The deinstallation is given almost as much attention as installation, with cleanup and returning the land to at least its original condition, if not better. For *Surrounded Islands*, 1980-83, in Florida, workers removed forty tons of garbage from the eleven islands before starting installation.

Christo and Jeanne-Claude perceive their work as environmental art, not land art, since they use sites that are already used and managed by people, rather than in wilderness areas. They want people to experience their installations as a "work of art of joy and beauty," without any deeper meaning. There is much to learn about the results of perseverance when considering Christo and Jeanne-Claude's commitment to their vision and the resulting beauty of the work.

Another example of environmental art might be *The Land of Giants*, a proposal by Choi+Shine Architects. These high voltage towers, shaped like walking men with their arms outstretched, won a 2008 design competition run by Iceland's power company. The legs of the figures could be configured in different ways, such as squatting on their knees, to accommodate the typography of the land. While the Iceland power company decided not to take up the proposal, *The Land of Giants* received a lot of publicity for the architects, while certainly opening up the public's mind to what is possible. As Jin Choi, one half of Choi+Shine partnership, says "So let's disguise the infrastructure, let's try to make it art instead of burying it, and make it stand out, like a monument." Surely the designers were disappointed when their project was not built, but their efforts have brought them many new opportunities for using their creativity.

Graffiti

Through their illegal writings and drawings on public walls, subway cars, and other surfaces, the hip hop culture of the late 1970's exposed the tremendous artistic talent of a few disenfranchised young people to a larger population. Armed with paint spray cans that can be easily hidden in clothing and backpacks, these kids created an art form that is now celebrated in museums, on apparel, and in sanctioned galleries, such as the HOPE Outdoor Gallery in Austin, TX.

Figure 10.5 HOPE Outdoor Gallery, Austin, TX, October 2014.

The Gallery is the brainchild of Andi Scull Cheatham, who saw possibilities in the abandoned three-story concrete walls left over from a failed condominium project on a hill surrounded by weeds, trash, and poison ivy. She was able to convince the owners, Vic Ayad and his partner, to let her use the land for a graffiti park. With the help of a lot of friends, the hillside property was cleared of trash and weeds for a 2011 opening as a free-for-all graffiti park.

Today it is the gathering place for anyone who wants to express his or her creativity with a spray can. As one of the artists Bob Wallace (aka Daddy Otis) said "(P)eople get to see your stuff and you can build a name, build a following." Ayad, who continues to own the land, spends $75,000 annually on taxes, etc., to keep the effort going. He says "But on the day it becomes economically unfeasible, I hope everyone looks at it as I do. Which is, instead of being sad that it's gone, we're all happy that it ever happened." That Zen attitude needs to be shared by all the artists using the Gallery, since no one controls where one can paint. An artist might spend hours on a piece to have it sprayed over by the next day. When Deathfox found his detailed mural of a feather headdress defaced, he philosophically responded "It's like an exercise in detachment." Thus is the life of a public artist, where so little can be controlled.

Yarn Bombing

Like most other graffiti, wrapping the urban landscape in knitting or crochet is often done without permission of the property owners. Since 2003, the artist Crocheted Olek (Poland, b. 1978) has crocheted full-bodied costumes for her street performances and and high-profile objects like buses and the bronze bull on Wall Street. Sometimes her work is sanctioned by a museum, but her unauthorized piece on the *Charging Bull* was ripped off in two hours by a park caretaker. Olek sees herself as an Artist, and says "If someone calls my bull a yarn bomb, I get really upset" and "Not everyone's work deserves to be in public."

Magda Sayeg (American, b. 1974) brings a more populist *joie de vivre* to the public display of knitting and crochet. In 2005, she knitted a blue-and-pink cozy for the door handle on the Houston boutique she co-owned.

Figure 10.6 Oak Forest Stitch and Bitch group, Yarn Bombing, Stevens Elementary School, Houston, Texas, 2013. Photography by Janice Daniel McKeehan.

People made a fuss over it, and she followed with a leg warmer for a stop sign and other "tags" around Houston. Other knitters joined her and they formed a group, called Knitta Please. By 2007 there were eleven members.

She closed her shop in 2009 and moved to Austin, where she is now earning major commissions. Toyota asked her to wrap a Prius and the City of Brooklyn contracted her to wrap sixty-nine parking meters. She can now charge $25,000 to $70,000 for a project. Sayeg has five assistants to operate knitting machines, rather than knitting by hand. She says "Focus on what you're good at, and if you can let go of your ego, outsource the rest." She isn't against using vintage afghans when she finds them, rather than creating everything from scratch, and she prefers acrylic yarns in her projects because the colors tend to be brighter and costs lower.

In 2011, Sayeg installed *Knitted Wonderland* in the plaza outside the Blanton Museum of Art in Austin. The idea originated with Jennifer Garner, the museum's Manager of School and Family Programs. One hundred and seventy-five knitters around Austin contributed, including students at The Girls School of Austin, who incorporated the proportions within a Fibonacci series into their designs. The knitters and museum volunteers wrapped the trees in time for Austin's biggest event, the SXSW music, film and interactive festival. While *Knitted Wonderland* was only up for three

Innovative Weaving

weeks, it brought a record number of visitors to the museum. Clearly, fiber art when presented in an unexpected environment and with enough publicity can have a significant impact.

On a smaller scale, the Oak Forest Stitch and Bitch group surprised Houston's Stevens Elementary School students as they returned from spring break in 2012. The schoolyard's trees were wrapped in colorful handwork and the fences held crocheted and knitted flowers and insects. (See Figure 10.6.)

With its air of subversion, yarnbombing seems to bring a sense of joy to both the maker and the viewer. Surely the intention is not that far from graffiti, yet the fact that it isn't destructive allows us to appreciate it more fully. The sense of surprise, seeing it so out of place.

Sculpture

While sculpture may be the oldest form of public art, the concept of standard large prefabricated shapes placed around a city and decorated by various artists is quite new. Started in 1986 in Zurich, Switzerland, with fiberglass cows, the city used the idea again in 1998 as a fundraising, with an auction of the cow sculptures at the end of the exhibition. The concept made its way to Chicago in 1999. As of 2015, there have been at least six such exhibitions in Asia, forty-five in Europe, and eighty-nine in North America, including 100 donkeys and 100 elephants in Washington, DC, Adirondack chairs in Vermont, and guitars in Austin.

Gibson Guitars Corp. sponsored 35 10-foot-tall fiberglass guitars as part of Austin Guitartown Project in 2007. The resulting auction brought in $589,000 for Health Alliance for Austin Musicians and three other charities. A few Guitartown guitars remain around the city, including eight on display at the Austin-Bergstrom International Airport.

Like any art project, successful or not, there are critics. In Washington, DC in 2002, the Green Party attempted to block Party Animals on free-speech grounds. They believed their sunflower symbol should also be represented, along with the elephants and donkeys. The alternative newspaper, the Washington City Paper, ran a story by Tom Scocca on May 17, 2002, questioning the value of the whole project:

> There are only so many things you do with a 4-foot-tall fiberglass animal. Three things, really: You can treat it like a wall and paint a mural on it, you can glue something decorative to its surface, and you can dress it up as something else. There may be other artistic options—smash it to rubble with a sledgehammer, put it in a galvanized trough and invite passers-by to urinate on it—but those lie outside the scope of the project.

Figure 10. 7 Tracie Sutton, *Piece of My Heart*, 2007. Austin-Bergstrom Airport. For Gibson Guitartown Project.

While art elitists might take such a view of the "CowParade" concept, it continues to be a popular way to raise funds for local charities, involve many community artists, and liven up the cityscape.

Meeting Ten: Weaving for the Public

Janet Echelman (American, b. 1966) provides a completely different approach to sculpture in the city. Her lacy aerial netting, suspended high from buildings by wires, changes shape with the breezes. First inspired by fishermen nets in India, her massive sculptures are often made by an industrial fishnet machine. Her piece *1.26 Sculpture Project* at the Amsterdam Light Festival (Figure 10.8) was hung over the Amstel River from December 2012 through January 2013. Echelman used NASA and NOAA data from the 2010 Chile earthquake, which resulted in the 1.26-microsecond shortening of the Earth's day, to design the sculpture that reflects the enormous tsunami waves that followed.

Figure 10.8 Janet Echelman, *1.26*, Amsterdam, 2012-2013. Photography by Martina McAuley under CC BY 2.0.

Made of a polyethylene fiber fifteen times stronger than steel and lit by an undulating projection system, the sculpture created reflections on the river that the Amsterdam Light Festival curator described as providing "more meaning to public spaces, showed the beauty of simplicity, and—probably most importantly—brought people together."

Figure 10.9 John Grade, "Host," 2008. Kaibab National Forest, Arizona. Ground seeds, rice pulp, capsicum, methylcellusole. Photography courtesy of the artist.

Rather than mitigating the forces of nature, sculptor John Grade (American, b. 1970) embraces decay. In 2008, he installed *Host* (Figure 10.9) in a recently burned out section of the Kaibab National Forest in Arizona. Made of ground seeds, rice pulp, and the non-toxic thickener methyl cellulose, the sculpture was intended to be eaten by the birds. However few remained in the fire-damaged area and the piece was moved to a green Aspen grove, where the squirrels took over the tasty sculpture, preventing birds from getting to it. When capsicum or pepper paste was painted on to deter the squirrels, the sculpture had an opportunity to deteriorate as Grade intended.

Tom Otterness (American, b. 1952) is considered one of the most prolific of American public artists. Coincidently, forty pieces of his work were on exhibition throughout Grand Rapids during the HGA Convergence conference in 2006. His sculptures, while appearing cheerful and cartoon-

Figure 10.10 Tom Otterness, *Life Underground*. 14th Street and 8th Ave A Train Station, New York City, 2002. Photography by Zen Skillicorn under CC BY 2.0.

119

Innovative Weaving

like, usually address capitalism, sex, and race issues. The Grand Rapids cast-bronze rounded stylized figures were similar to those in his 2002 installation called *Life Underground*, located in the 14th Street—Eighth Avenue New York City subway station, took over 10 years to complete. Otterness put a lot of time into exploring creative locations for his figures, while accommodating the rules of the station design.

Otterness had a major crash in his popularity when a journalist wrote in 2004 that the sculptor, as an expression of punk art in 1977 had himself filmed tying a shelter dog to a tree, shooting it, and watching it die. The story grew. Otterness issued a public apology in 2008, but his major projects started to fall apart by 2011 as municipal art commissions began to receive pressure from those angered and offended by the punk film.

In response to the film, Andrew Tider, who teaches Ethical Creativity at City University of New York, illegally and anonymously installed *Life Underground +3* in the same subway station as *Life Underground*. The parody is comprised of three figures in the style of Otterness, one holds a gun aimed at a dog and a third stands by taking a picture. Time will tell if the controversial sculptor's career will be able to recover from such negative publicity.

As weavers and guild members, we have much to learn from all of the public artists in this chapter. Perseverance is certainly one of them, but also consideration of the various forms possible for public art and the acceptance of the ephemeral nature of their work, which is particularly important for us fiber artists.

Developing a Public Project for Your Guild

Whether temporary or permanent, small or large, you will likely find that you need time, skills, and financial resources outside the capability of the guild for a public project. The following questions should help you consider whether you and your guild are ready for such an effort. The answers can be the start of the information you will need for any funding or approval requests, while also helping ensure the team stays focused on the initial goals.

- **Why are you doing a public art project?**
  A public project will take major resources of time and money. Is it worth it? What are the benefits for the guild and for the individual participants?

- **Who will plan and carry out the project?**
  Likely a team of guild members is needed. Who is on the team and who is the leader? What skills do you need and will those be paid or volunteer?

- **What is the story you want to tell?**
  This is essentially the artist statement, but must be written to show a connection to the community. The project needn't be literal or historical, but the more it relates to the town and community the more likely you are to get approval of the property owners and any other regulatory and funding agencies.

- **What is the form of the project?**
  Obviously the details will evolve, but will the project be fiber or will it represent fiber in a more permanent medium, such as tile or metal? Is it oversized? Generally what will it look like?

Meeting Ten: Weaving for the Public

- **Where do you want to install the project?**
  You might want to have alternatives, but certainly this answer will determine the approval process required and what might be necessary for installation.

- **How will the public interact with it?**
  Is it intended to be touched? Does the public merely look? What happens to the piece if they do touch or manhandle it? Do you mitigate damage or see its destruction as part of the process?

- **How much will the project cost?**
  Early in the development process this is certainly an approximate number. But in order to get very far, you need to determine if you need outside money.

All of these answers will likely be needed in any approval process and funding requests for a public project. If you have a project that demonstrates an understanding of the challenges involved and one that connects with the interests of the community, you may find that there are several sources for funding:

City Public Art Programs

Many towns around North America now support public art through various programs, such as the City of Austin's Art in Public Places that contributes 2% of the estimated construction budget for art inside and outside city buildings. The website Publicartist.org is a place to enter your information and then receive announcements of public art projects all over the country.

Figure 10.11 Yuliya Lanina, "Earth Mother." October 1-November 31, 2015. Ramsey Park, Austin, TX.

Airports are certainly an opportunity to display public art. A recent call for artwork for a walkway at the Austin-Bergstrom International Airport received 129 applications. While a $2 million art project for the airport entrance and $1 million for another in the airport expansion seems nothing but terrifying, it is worthwhile to keep an eye on smaller, more doable public art projects for the guild, such as at a local library.

The City of Austin has taken on another program specific to temporary public art called Tempo that might be quite appropriate for textiles. In the spring 2015, the City put out a call for temporary art to be installed in parks and other municipal sites. Ten projects were selected, including *Earth Mother* by Yuliya Lanina (Figure 10.10), made of recycled Styrofoam and live plants. None of the pieces were up for more than six months. Such a temporary exhibition might be perfect for a fiber project.

National Endowment for the Arts

An NEA grant is more competitive than a local one, but may be worth considering. NEA is looking for specific events and activities that will make a difference in a community or field. As of 2015, grants for art works by organizations are given:

> To support the creation of art that meets the highest standards of excellence, public engagement with diverse and excellent art, lifelong learning in the arts, and the strengthening of communities through the arts. Matching grants generally range from $10,000 to $100,000.

Another category is "Our Town":

> Arts Engagement, Cultural Planning, and Design Projects that represent the distinct character and quality of their communities. These projects require a partnership between a nonprofit organization and a local government entity, with one of the partners being a cultural organization. Matching grants range from $25,000 to $200,000.

Books and even classes are now available to help you write a grant proposal and to manage the specific reporting requirements. It is worth exploring the NEA website, along with other grant-giving foundations specializing in the arts.

Crowdfunding

The practice of funding a project by raising many small amounts of money from a large number of people over the internet is relatively new, starting with ArtistShare in 2003. Today there are many sites, such as Kickstarter.com and Indiegogo.com. More specific to non-profits is Razoo.com, which allows any donation to a guild with non-profit status whether attached to a specific project or not.

Whichever way you go, at least one member of your guild, if not more, will need to commit to the fundraising effort. Just like the people working on the design, approval process, and construction of the project, the skills and perseverance of the fundraiser will determines its success.

Strengthening Up Your Perseverance

Whether working on a large public art project with your guild or on an individual weaving project, bringing it to fruition is dependent upon your perseverance, pushing past all that seems to be trying to stop you. Whether it is bureaucracy or problems with your warp's tension, a project depends upon your creative energy to bust through or around obstacles.

As simplistic as this might sound, that energy may be dependent upon the availability of the body chemical dopamine. In an intriguing article entitled "Neuroscience of Perseverance" in Psychology Today.com, December 26, 2011, Christopher Bergland, an endurance athlete, writes that dopamine is the fuel that keeps us motivated to persevere and achieve our goals. When we develop a habit of little successes, we are able to motivate ourselves to continue to pursue the "highs" created by dopamine. The release of the chemical is the internal reward system that nature has given us to help us survive as a species. It feels good to eat, mate, sleep, and push past obstacles. As individuals of the species, we can survive without jolts of dopamine, although it has to be boring as heck.

Based on the scientific research on dopamine, Bergland writes and lectures about developing habits to help people overcome lethargy and achieve their chosen goals. The following is a condensed version of his approach:

- **Breakdown a major goal into smaller tasks that you can complete as part of your day.** You need to feel you are moving toward your goal with one little success at a time. Bergland says "Being uninspired and lacking self-motivation is a downward spiral that can snowball out of control. Look at every thing you do in the day as a chance to create a sense of reward and deliver a rush of dopamine."

Meeting Ten: Weaving for the Public

- **Write down the list of the tasks with reasonable planned completion dates.** Each task should have a beginning, middle, and end, so that you can gain a sense of satisfaction as you work toward the goal. Checking off each task as you complete it gives you a sense of satisfaction and helps you see your progress. Adjust planned completion dates, if needed, and without being hard on yourself. Don't procrastinate and wait until the last minute to complete a task. A regular schedule of little successes is ultimately more satisfying than a "Whew! I barely made it."

- **Persevering through a difficult task boosts your self-confidence and feels good.** When you look forward to a feeling of success in the immediate future, no matter how small, you can focus less on any sense of drudgery. Giving up on an important task usually leaves you disappointed, dissatisfied, and possibly depressed. In other words, laziness isn't really easy.

- **Congratulate yourself each time you complete a task, particularly for one that presents a challenge for you.** Don't depend upon the praise of anyone else. Bergland says "Being self-congratulatory isn't about ego or hubris, it is about harnessing your reward circuitry and tapping your dopamine pipeline. If you neglect to consciously acknowledge that you have achieved a goal, dopamine will not be released and you will not reinforce the habit of perseverance."

These four habits can help you meet your personal weaving goals, but are needed even more when dealing with large community projects. Be inspired by artists, such as Christo and Jeanne-Claude, who see the many-year process of their projects as part of their art, not a barrier to it.

Exercises

These exercises are intended to help your guild (or yourself) develop a vision for a temporary or more permanent art project for your larger community.

Exercise 10.1 (30 minutes)

Ten Minutes What story might your guild tell about your community's use of textiles now or in the past? Write down as many ideas as possible.

Twenty Minutes One at a time, share two or three of your ideas with the group and note any subsequent ideas that come to mind.

Exercise 10.2 (30 minutes)

Ten Minutes How might you tell that story through a public art project? Be open to the possibilities of collaborating with other artists and craftspeople, such as painters and metal workers. Write down as many ideas as you can.

Twenty Minutes One at a time, share two or three of your ideas with the group and note any subsequent ideas that come to mind.

Conclusion

Exposing the maximum number of people to the work of weavers through public art brings many benefits to your guilds and to you as a weaver, such as furthering an appreciation of weaving and growing your guild. However any weaving project, particularly those at a scale of public art, demands perseverance to handle all the challenges to come. Insufficient funding, lengthy approval processes, limited labor resources, flagging enthusiasm of volunteers, and time constraints are only a few of the problems that are likely to arise. Only by accepting these as part of the process can you and your guild make a successful public art project not only in the eyes of the community, but within the group and your own view of the project.

Whether developing a large public project or one of your own, the habits of perseverance are worth considering to help you bring your creative visions to fruition. Time spent on higher priorities prevent all of us from dedicating as much time as we would like to weaving. But accomplishing little tasks toward the larger goal will help you feel like you are moving forward as a weaver.

Further Sources for Inspiration

Yarnbomb Consortium on Facebook

Publicartist.org for notification of projects

Web search of all the artists mentioned

MEETING ELEVEN: PICTURE IT IN MOTION

Consider how our eyes are unconsciously drawn to the slightest movement that comes into our field of vision. Moving pictures exploit that natural instinct. This chapter explores the techniques used in films, considered the most important art form of the 20th century, television, games, and other forms of moving pictures. You are encouraged to develop ways to create actual movement within a project or only design a perception of movement. As in the rest of this study guide, we provide the inspiration. How you execute your ideas is up to your own creativity.

In addition to artistic inspiration, these relatively new technologies have increased our ability to learn from weaving experts without leaving our homes, often at no cost. This chapter suggests a few of the resources that exploit moving pictures to teach weavers new skills and improve on the skills we have. Film and video can be both the source of inspiration for our work and the conduit for improving our ability to express that creativity.

A Very Brief History of Moving Pictures

As many of the challenges of still photography were overcome in the 1800's, innovators turned their efforts to making those images move. An early approach was to take advantage of the "persistence of vision" effect, which creates an illusion of movement, such as in a flipbook. The following table provides only a sliver of all the innovative ideas that have led to the sometimes overwhelming availability today of moving images and the technology to make them.

Figure 11.1 "Toy" praxinoscope. Industrial Development Limited. 2006

Date	Innovation	Innovator	Comment
1833 or 1834	Zoescope, spinning drum with slits. Still images around inside of drum	William George Horner, British	
1860s	Projection of Zoescope		Allowed more than one person at a time to see the movement.
1877	Praxinoscope, mirrors in the center of a moving drum with still images.	Charles-Émile Rynaud, French	See Figure 11.1. The drum is a rotating flat disk in this version
1895	First film using a Cinémagraphe, comprised of a camera, projector and film printer.	Auguste and Louis Lumière, French	
1902	Early narrative film *A Trip to the Moon* released	Georges Méliès, French	These early films were single reels lasting around 10 to 16 minutes.

Innovative Weaving

Date	Innovation	Innovator	Comment
1909	First instantaneous transmission of images	A. Fornier, French	Early form of television
1911	Multi-reel film, called features, became common.		More complex stories possible
1922	*The Toll of the Sea* is first Technicolor feature.		But technology too expensive and difficult for general use.
1927	Synchronized sound introduced in film *The Jazz Singer* with Al Jolson		
1929	*Gold Diggers of Broadway* film released using Technicolor.		Technology improved and more affordable.
1941	US adopts 525-line TV standard		
1944	Soviet Union develops 625-line TV standard, later implemented across Europe.		
1953	First wide-screen Cinemascope film *The Robe* released. Used aspect ratio of 2.66:1, rather than Academy standard of 1.37:1.	Spyros P. Skouras, Greece	Allowed close-ups without cutting out other characters and background.
1954	First US television broadcast in color, Tournament of Roses Parade.		
1960	Computer graphics invented	William Fetter, US, working for Boeing Aircraft as part of Department of Defense Cold War efforts	
1967	"Filmed inserts" used to promote record sales. Uses slow motion, reversing the film, and unusual camera angles for "Strawberry Fields Forever" and "Penny Lane" promos.	Peter Goldman, Swedish television director	Predecessor to music videos.
1968	First portable video camera and recorder, Sony Portapak.		Artists could produce moving pictures easily and quickly. Instant feedback.
1971	First coin-operated video game, *Computer Space*, introduced.		
1972	Atari's *Pong* introduced, a two-dimensional table tennis game.	Allan Alcorn, US	
1975	First home version of *Pong*, with console. Sold by Sears.		
1981	MTV begins showing music videos 24 hours a day.		
1999	First commercial mobile videophone, Kyocera VP-210 Visual Phone.		
2005	YouTube.com started as a method of sharing videos	Chad Hurley (US), Steve Chen (Taiwan), and Jawed Karim (Germany)	By 2013, 1 billion users were going to the site every month.

The Different Forms of Moving Pictures

We have come a long way from the days when the only way to see a picture move was to thumb through a flipbook or imagining the eyes in a portrait were following you. All of the examples of

Meeting Eleven: Picture It In Motion

moving pictures presented below deserve your further exploration. Watch the films and search for clips on YouTube. Only when you see the actual movement will the importance of these innovators become apparent. As you watch, consider ways that you might add actual or a perception of movement to your own woven projects.

Feature Film

Narrative and documentary films, intended for a theater audience, are called features. In order to allow two showings an evening, these generally run about ninety minutes in length. Although still called "film," many are now in a digital format.

Today feature films are almost always produced only when they are expected to make many millions of dollars. There is always a tension between art (the filmmaker) and commercial value (the studios in control of the money). Artists in Hollywood have often suffered as they attempted to be true to their work. One of those artists was the avant-garde filmmaker Oskar Fischinger (German, 1900-1967). Before he worked in LA, he was an innovator in abstract musical animation. His *Raumlichtkunst (Space Light Art),* consisting of abstract images projected on three different screens, was first performed in Germany in 1926. In 2012, the work was reconstructed and exhibited at the Whitney Museum and Tate Modern, London.

Fischinger was brought in to design the J.S. Bach's *Toccata and Fugue in D Minor* sequence in Walt Disney's *Fantasia* (1940). He used his abstract aesthetic for the Disney project, but left the production when the Disney studio altered his designs to include realistic images of the musicians, which he saw as compromising his abstract vision. Despite the modifications, the segment is considered the most interesting and innovative of the whole film.

Monty Python animator and director Terry Gilliam (American, b. 1940) fought even harder to preserve his artistic vision from the changes demanded by Universal Studios in 1985. His *Brazil* shows a distorted world run by heartless bureaucrats in the most inefficient ways possible. The only escape is one's own dream world. He used a wide-angle lens from high and low angles to distort faces, yet insure that the background is expanded and in sharp focus.

When Universal shortened the film for US distribution from its two-hour, twenty-two-minute length and cut scenes at the end to make a happy ending, Gilliam went rogue and screened his version without studio approval for Los Angeles students and critics. After *Brazil* won the Los Angeles Film Critics award for Best Picture, Universal allowed Gilliam to supervise a 132-minute version for release. Gilliam says " I don't mind failing on my own terms, I just don't want to fail on someone else's terms."

Another innovator Akira Kurosawa (Japan, 1910-1998) directed thirty films in his 57-year career. His techniques have influenced filmmakers all over the world. His innovative approaches to telling a story are described in a YouTube.com video by Tony Zhou called "Composing Movement." Watch any of Kurosawa's films, such as *Ran* and *Seven Samurai*, and study how he uses the following to control tension:

> *Weather* Falling rain and the effects of wind are backdrops for what might otherwise be stagnant scenes.
>
> *Groups* The movement of crowds of people help raise the emotional level of a scene. A hundred angry people certainly has more power than one.

Innovative Weaving

Individuals Exaggerated, unrealistic placement of characters create heightened interest. Individualized gestures, such as a limp or twitch, contribute to quick identification of characters from different angles.

Camera Movement Fluid, unbroken movements of the camera. His camera shots had something different happening with a beginning, middle, and end in its action.

Movement of Cut When the film cuts from one image to another, a movement appears to match that in the next cut, although the rhythm usually changes. Thus a relatively still movement morphs into more action and then back to a slower pace.

See also the link in the Further Sources for Inspiration at the end of the chapter for a reference to a similar analysis of Hollywood director Steven Spielberg's innovative filmmaking techniques.

Opening Credits

The title sequences at a film's beginning list the key production people, cast members, and financial backers, as well as set the atmosphere for the beginning scenes. Saul Bass (American, 1920-1996) brought abstract modernism, to the titles, such as his work at the beginning of *The Man with the Golden Arm* in 1955. During the opening credits, different configurations of long thin white rectangles appear on a black screen, ending with an abstracted tortured white hand and forearm.

It is worth watching the YouTube.com video of Kyle Cooper talking about the history of titles and the innovative work of Saul Bass in the eight-minute *The Look of Saul Bass*, TCM, 2004. Some say his work influenced all modern opening title sequences, particularly the AMC series *Mad Men*.

Leanne Shapton (Canada, b. 1973) created a series of black watercolors using stills from films, such as Bass's titles for *The Man with the Golden Arm*, in her book *Sunday Night Movies*, 2013. Her website describes her work as follows:

> She captures fragments and stills that appeared on the screen for mere seconds,...forging haunting images that stay with you, much like a hazy but stubborn recollection of dreams past.... This journey through Shapton's film life becomes a wistful, if light-handed, celebration of the quiet moments in life, which too often slip by unnoticed. Each painting is like a love letter to the art of cinema.

Avant-Garde Film

In the 1920's film became a medium for experimental expression by avant-garde artists such as Marcel Duchamp, Jean Cocteau, and Man Ray. Rather than telling a linear story, they saw their work closer to poetry, where events didn't need to link to each other. They embraced abstract images, exploring time, movement, and sound. Their films were low budget, with possibly only the filmmaker as crew.

You can watch experimental films on YouTube.com, such as *Ballet Mécanique* by Fernand Léger and Len Lye's *A Colour Box* (1935) with shapes painted directly on celluloid. You can also attend festivals where short-format programs present the most innovative ideas in film.

Video Art

Nam June Paik (South Korea, 1931-2006) is considered the father of video art or what is more recently designated "time-based media art." In 1963, he experimented with television sets, using magnets to distort the images of shows during broadcast. Possibly of most interest to weavers is the piece he did at the end of his life entitled *Ommah*. A transparent traditional boy's robe hangs in front of an LCD television monitor playing a video of three Korean-American girls in traditional dress dancing, playing ball, and beating a drum. In the background are images of old video games and television shows. The music is ambient studio sounds and Paik's experimental tapes from the 1950s.

Figure 11.2 Nam June Paik, *Ommah*, 2005. Silk robe, 19-inch LCD monitor. National Gallery of Art. Photography by Sarah Stierch under CC by 2.0.

Another example of video art is an early work by Kehinde Wiley (American, b. 1977) called *Smile* (2001). The one-and-a-half-hour student video played during the exhibit of his super-sized hyper-naturalistic portraits at the Ft. Worth Modern Museum of Art. His paintings are usually of African-Americans posed in the style of the Old Masters with repeated patterning as background. In the video, four faces of different young black men appear on the screen at once. Each had been asked simply to smile at the camera for an hour. After a while, it became more difficult to continue the happy face, and their efforts turn to an endurance test. The intention seems to reveal the challenge of keeping up a false front.

Each of these artists used video to communicate an artistic concept of transition through time. Movement wasn't merely "nice to have." It was essential for telling the story.

Television

A "vast wasteland" is how Newton N. Minow, FCC Chairman, described television in 1961. And it still is not the place where visual artists flock for freedom of expression. To begin with, it is the only one of the moving picture forms we look at that is regulated by the Federal Communication Commission (FCC). That responsibility is intended to protect the public from obscene and indecent material and ensure that programming is politically balanced. Thus broadcast television corporations are highly adverse to risk out of fear of losing their license to operate or incur large fines. When you consider that in 1957, CBS pulled the pilot episode of *Leave It To Beaver* because it showed the boys hiding a pet alligator in a toilet, it becomes clear that the studios have pushed those limits enormously since the early years of television. In the case of the Beaver, a compromise was met with the agreement to show a part of the toilet but not the seat.

While examples of creative geniuses tortured by the corporate censors abound, there is also much to learn from the geniuses that knew how to work around that risk aversion and continue to express their creativity. The writer and director Norman Lear, originator of *All in the Family*, is one of those pioneers that somehow knew how to manage discussion of very sensitive cultural and political issues by allowing his characters to be the worst of bigots, while also making the audience laugh.

Cable and the internet have the luxury of not being regulated by the FCC, allowing both to explore a wider range of content, obviously for the better and worse. But of the Emmy nominations in 2015, only 188 were for the five major broadcast networks (ABC, CBS, NBC, FOX, and CW), while 316 were for 33 cable networks led by HBO, AMC, and Comedy Central. Global provider of streaming film and television Netflix had 34 nominations and Amazon had 12. Five internet sites, such as LouisCK.net and FunnyorDie.com, had seven nominations. As alternatives to the risk adverse broadcast television networks, these cable and internet sources are succeeding because people crave innovation and artists are driven to provide it.

In 2015, Brenda Lawrence created a list of *Seventeen TV Shows That will Spark Your Creativity* (http://www.brit.co/creative-tv-show/). The first six on the list below are from Lawrence, followed by a few additional recommendations:

- *Flight of the Conchords* (HBO, Netflix.com) New Zealand musical duo come to the States to make it big. Rampant silliness and inventive animations.

- *Writers Room* (Sundance, Hulu.com) What inspired some TV shows and some of the major plot decisions.

- *American Genius* (National Geographic, Hulu.com) How rivalries seems to spark creativity.

- *Iconoclasts* (Sundance.tv, Amazon) Passions and motivations of people like Lena Dunham, Judd Apatow, Seth MacFarlane, and Norah Jones

- American Masters (PBS.org) Creative arts and their impact on American pop culture.

- *Project Runway* (Lifetime, Hulu.com) Reality TV silliness, but worth watching designers whip up outfits and hearing judges' comments.

- *Craft in America* (PBS.org) Profiles of craftspeople, including weavers Randall Darwall, Lia Cook, and Consuelo Jimenez Underwood.

- *On Story* (PBS.com) Interviews with directors and screenwriters during the Austin Film Festival, where they discuss their inspirations and artistic decisions.

Television also allows us to watch creative innovation in the choreography of dancers, such as Derek Hough, on NBC's *Dancing with the Stars,* and in the art direction on cable shows like *Justified* and *Game of Thrones*. Yet another source is in the inventiveness of commercials. The Association of Independent Commercial Producers puts on a show every year at the Museum of Modern Art in New York to celebrate the art and technique of American commercials. One of the videos at the 2016 exhibit was the "2016 Sponsor Reel—Dir Cut " submitted by Method Design, who described the work as "Motion capture, procedural animation and dynamic simulations combine to create a milieu of iconic pop dance moves that become an explosion of colorful fur, feathers, particles and more." See the video at http://design.methodstudios.com. Yes, television may continue to seem like a wasteland, but there is more than enough inspiration in a few oases to keep us all busy.

Games

"Video games" are those that are played on a console, such as Playstation and Xbox, or at an arcade, while "computer games," are played on a home computer. A 1983-1985 crash in the video game industry, caused by oversaturation, led to many development companies going into bankruptcy or restructuring. The result was the increased popularity of computer gaming.

Cory Arcangel (American, b. 1978), has based much of his work on hacking into existing computer games to create art. For instance, his *Various Self Playing Bowling Games* was exhibited simultaneously at the Whitney Museum in New York on six screens and Barbarian Art Space in London on 14 screens in 2011. Each screen had a different version of a bowling game from different companies, such as the earliest and most Pong-like Atari Bowling and Nintendo Game Cube-Strike Force Bowling, played in a loop. Arcangel's genius becomes apparent when the viewer realizes that each game has been reprogrammed to only throw gutter balls. No one wins. See YouTube.com for videos of his hacks.

While there are plenty of action-based games available today, some quite brutal, there are nonviolent alternatives, based on skill-building that have put aesthetics as a high priority. *Monument Valley* by ustwo is such a game. Developed by Ken Wong, this Apple iPad app consists of optical illusion mazes influenced by Japanese prints, M.C. Escher, and minimalist sculpture. Wong wanted each frame to be able to stand alone for public display.

Named Apple's best iPad game for 2014, *Monument Valley* uses exquisite color combinations and intriguing angles and textures. If you haven't been motivated to try out any computer game yet, consider that there just might be some that will get you thinking about an unusal idea for a weaving.

Short-Format Videos

The short format of videos, whether intended to sell something, like music or beer, or tell a short story, provides the perfect medium for visual

Figure 11.3 Ken Wong, designer. Monument Valley, ustwo, 2013.

artists to experiment with movement and time. A fascinating music video on Youtube.com, *We Got Time* by Moray McLaren, uses the praxinoscope. (See Figure 11.1.) You can also watch a "Making of" video by the video's designer, David Wilson. The video shows the technique he used to match up the images with the rate of the film.

Likely will come a day when research shows the explosion of creativity that occurred after the launch of YouTube in 2005. Today we have immediate access to innovations all over the world, along with different points of view and styles found in different cultures. The gift is that we can never run out of short videos to inspire our work. The curse is, of course, we may spend so much time on YouTube.com that we never get around to expressing our own creativity.

Light Shows

While often performed live, rather than recorded for replay, the visuals shown at dance parties and clubs to accompany music are worth considering for a weaving exhibition. Liquid light shows were popular in the 1960s to accompany electronic music and avant-garde theatre performances. They then were adapted to rock and psychedelic music. Colored mineral oil and alcohol were placed on a slide heated by a lamp to produce changing color patterns when projected.

Innovative Weaving

Figure 11.4 Steve Wechsler and Inga Marie Carmel. Slide for Blammo! light show, 1992. Courtesy of the artists.

While light shows evolved into elaborate productions of great complexity, including the use of lasers, do-it-yourself visuals were popular at underground or warehouse parties to accompany electronic music in the 1990s. Blammo! was an Austin production group that used three slide projectors with still images filtered through a color wheel made of theatrical gels and rotated with an egg beater controlled by a rheostat. Black and white images were Xeroxed onto acetate, sometimes colored, and mounted in slide blanks.

Your Weaving in Motion

In the chapter for Meeting Five, we discussed the importance of balance in architecture, but there is a lot of power achieved when you intentionally create imbalance in your work. The illusion of motion, such as the anticipation of something falling or traveling from one place to another creates tension and helps tell a story.

Actual Movement

The easiest way to create movement in your weaving is to make something to wear and let the body facilitate motion. Iris van Herpen (Dutch, 1984) uses 3-D printers to create dresses and shoes that express her interest in attraction and repulsion. One of the dresses from her "Wilderness Embodied" haute couture collection for Fall 2013 had weeping willow-like branches extending almost two feet from the model's body, light enough to bounce as she walked.

Possibly this piece might be a little too much movement for the office? When you consider drape of yardage for a dress, you are envisioning its movement on the body. Will the dress stand away from the body and move stiffly through space? Or will it undulate with the movement of the wearer as she walks?

The technology of e-textiles provides a way to weave moving light into your piece. Inga Marie Carmel, one of our WSSA members, has woven conductive thread with ramie and linen and incorporated LED lights to simulate a beating heart in her wall piece *<3*.

Carmel programmed a Lily Pad circuit board on the back of her piece to flash LED lights at the speed of a heartbeat. See Figure 11.6. She used three layers of felt to separate the conductive threads, thus preventing them from crossing each other and shorting out.

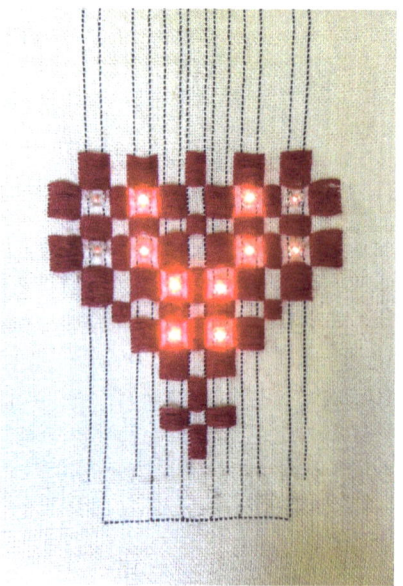

Figure 11.5 Inga Marie Carmel. "< 3". 2011. Ramie and linen, LED paranha square lights, conductive thread, Lily Pad board. Courtesy of the artist.

Meeting Eleven: Picture It In Motion

Lynn Bruning hosts a blog at etextilelounge.com that is filled with ideas for adding light to your weaving. Also see Further Sources for Inspiration at the end of the chapter.

Figure 11.6 Inga Marie Carmel. "<3". Back view. Courtesy of the artist.

Perceived Movement

All this actual movement might be fun for a short-term exhibition or for apparel, but the incorporation of the perception of movement might be more appropriate for weaving projects. Consider the following techniques:

> *Left to Right Line* A line that moves from left to right to some sort of payoff works well for those of us who read Western languages. The line is perceived as a speed line or trail.
>
> *Op Art* Repetitive hard-edged curving lines can seem to vibrate as they blur and create optical ripples. Consider some of the twill patterns in books like *A Weaver's Book of 8-Shaft Patterns* by Carol Strickler that you may have previously passed by because they seemed too active or "hard on the eyes." Used judiciously, one may be just what you need to liven up a design.

Anticipated Movement

Our past experience leads us to imagine that things will fall from a height or a particular motion results in a following motion, such as a hammer raised as if to strike. In the untitled 1966 lithograph, Robert Motherwell (American, 1915-1991) demonstrated how much movement can be implied within a two-dimensional still image.

Figure 11.7 Robert Motherwell. Untitled, 1966. Lithograph on paper image. 19x13 in. Society for the Arts, Religion, and Contemporary Culture (Published). Smithsonian American Art Museum, 1976.108.88

Cropped Figure Cutting off part of an object at the edge of a piece gives the illusion that it is either entering or leaving the frame.

Repeated Figure Using the same image, but modified, over and over can create a sense of motion and passing time. This might be an opportunity for a triptych, with each panel showing an object in different positions across the piece. The wall piece by Stephan Balkenhol (German, b. 1957) entitled *4 Figures*, 2000, at the Modern Art Museum of Fort Worth, is comprised of four carved wood men on platforms in painted black slacks and white buttoned-down shirts. The group seems to show the passage of time, the one most to the left is turned outward, the next one is turned straight ahead, the next one a little to the right, and the last one on the right is turned toward the right. The relative positioning of the figures seems to create a sense of movement and the passage of time.

Blurred Outlines Some overshot patterns almost vibrate with the blurred effect of the half tones and the sharp edges of the weft floats, such as "Pioneer Trail" in Marguerite Porter Davison's *A Handweavers Pattern Book*. Used in the right place, one of these active patterns might be what you need to spice up a design.

Learning Visually

Not only can we be inspired by the art of moving pictures, but the advancement in technology provides opportunities for us to share and learn the craft of weaving never available before. The more complex a technique, the more difficult it is to effectively describe in a book of words and still images. On the other hand, a craft like spinning might not be complex, but is nearly impossible to explain. If you know the basics of spinning on a wheel, watch the video *Spin Cotton from Seed* by wandagrayson646 (January 8, 2011) on YouTube.com, and you will say "I can do that." Observing hands in motion, along with the ability to watch the video repeatedly until we get it, surely is contributing to the advancement of all fiber crafts, including weaving.

The following are only a few examples of the wealth of information to be mined in current moving picture technology:

Television

While there seem to be plenty of television shows about quilting and sewing, weaving doesn't seem to warrant one. Until that changes, *Project Runway* on Lifetime might be the only show somewhat related to what we do. The second episode of Season 13, "Unconventional Movie Night," required the participants to made outfits from stuff collected from a movie theater, including rolls of tickets, straws, and dvds. If you can handle the reality TV silliness, there is much to glean from watching the designers work and the judges' comments. While you might not agree with the judges, they are the industry gatekeepers and their negative viewpoints prevent these people from being in the final fashion show at Fashion Week and winning money to start their own design business. As top designers and fashion magazine editors, they are experienced in what sells and what doesn't. Certainly it would be better to see more about the design and construction process and less about who is being brought to tears. It is inspirational (and frustrating) to see how quickly experienced designers can pull something together.

Downloadable Videos

Publishers seem to be moving away from hard-cover books to different electronic formats, including downloads from the internet. Certainly this makes for instant gratification for us when we run into a stumbling block in a project. Videos can be downloaded from Interweavestore.com, such as Tom Knisely's *The Weaver's Yarn Companion*. Weavolution.com has a "cyber-fiber online classroom" where you can access *Color and Inspiration* by Daryl Lancaster. You can sign up for live webinars or purchase them after the fact. You can also order instructional DVDs from Handweavers Guild of America, like Sara Lamb's *Spin to Weave*. Your access to technical expertise has never been as expansive as it is today.

YouTube.com

While all the videos described above have purchase prices, the videos on YouTube are almost always free. Two examples are Jette Vandermeiden's *Weaving Basics: Making a Warp* and *Spin Cotton from Seed* by wandagrason646 (Jan 8, 2011). Both provide free, repeatable access to information that can best be understood through moving pictures. YouTube is certainly the most economical and quickest way to research weaving techniques, and there seems to be an endless number of weavers anxious to share their knowledge.

Exercises

The following exercises encourage you to think about how you might incorporate movement into your work, either actual movement or only a perception of it. If the book *Motion Graphic Design* by John Krasner is available from the library or other sources, you are encouraged to use the dvd in the back to help stimulate ideas. However the exercises should work just fine without the book.

Exercise 11.1 (30 minutes)

Ten Minutes If *Motion Graphic Design*, 3rd edition, by Jon Krasner is available: Watch Chapter 7 on the dvd in the back of *Motion Graphic Design* (6 minutes). Write down ideas that you might be able to bring to your weaving. If the *Motion Graphic Design* dvd is not available: List your favorite movies? Select one or two and consider how you might interpret that in a weaving.

Twenty Minutes One at a time, share two or three of your ideas with the group and note any subsequent ideas that come to mind.

Exercise 11.2 (30 minutes)

Ten Minutes Expand on your idea in Exercise 11.1 by adding further motion, either actual or perceived, to your piece.

Twenty Minutes One at a time, share two or three of your ideas with the group and note any subsequent ideas that come to mind.

Conclusion

The relatively new world of moving pictures provides a wealth of inspiration for weavers. Open your eyes and creativity to the new technology and design aesthetics. Some of you will want to jump into learning new skills, while most of you will find opportunities to stretch your imagination and incorporate innovative ideas that fit well into your own aesthetic and current capabilities. And take advantage of all the videos available today to help you improve your technical skills or learn new ones.

Innovative Weaving

Further Sources for Inspiration

Adafruit.com Do-it-yourself electronics.

Betancourt, Michael. *The History of Motion Graphics from Avant-Garde to Industry in the United States.* Wildside Press, 2013.

Etextilelounge.com. Lynn Bruning's blog of ideas for adding electronics to wearables.

Expanded Cinema: Art, Performance, Film. Edited by A.L. Rees, Duncan White, Steven Ball and David Curtis. London: Tate Publishing, 2011.

Free Radicals; A history of experimental film. 2011. DVD

Giannetti, Louis and Scott Eyman. *Flashback; a brief history of film.* Boston: Allyn & Bacon, 2010.

Krasner, Jon. *Motion graphic design; applied history and aesthetics*, 3rd edition. Burlington, MA: Focal Press, 2013. Watch dvd in the back.

LAvideoFilmmaker.com. Steven Spielberg Film Techniques—With pretty pictures.

MEETING TWELVE: INSTALLATION ART AND LEGACY

Installation seems the most appropriate art form to conclude this book on creativity. All the types of works we have explored can be and have been incorporated into installations, particularly music, sculpture, painting, video, and performance. But this relatively new expression not only pulls different art forms into one work, but also asks people inside to be more than just a watcher, but a participant. Rather than it being created to last "for the ages," an installation usually is temporary and built for only one location, not to be sold or moved somewhere else, making the time spent there more precious. Photographs, videos, the written word, and memories are often the only legacy remaining, which leads to the question, "What will your own work leave behind?" This last chapter gives you an opportunity to think about what you would like the viewer to take from your work.

A Very Brief History of Installation Art

While transforming an entire space into a work of art occurred earlier, it was the late 1960s and early 1970s when the practice flowered into an art form, along with theories about it, as exemplified here:

> (I)nstallation art posits us as both centred and decentred, and this conflict is itself decentring since it structures an irresolvable antagonism between the two. Installation art calls for a self-present viewing precisely in order to subject him/her to the process of fragmentation. When successful, this involves an overlap between the philosophical model of subjectivity presupposed by the work and the production of this model in the literal viewer who experiences it first hand. By this means, installation art aims not only to problematise the subject as decentred, but also to produce it.

If you find this paragraph enlightening, you are encouraged to read Clair Bishop's thorough history of the art form's development, *Installation Art*. For those of you that are befuddled, we are going to approach the topic more simplistically. Installation art is three-dimensional, site-specific, and usually transforms an interior space, rather than outdoors. Many such works invite the spectator into the piece and expect some sort of involvement.

The precursor to installation art is usually said to be *The Merzbau* (1923-1936) created by Kurt Schwitters (Germany, 1887-1948), whose work was influenced by Dada and Surrealism. He started as a post-Impressionist, but the turbulent times following WWI led him to Dadaism. In 1923, Schwitters began to transform six rooms in his parent's Hanover house into a sculptural environment. He created white angled surfaces that protruded into the rooms, creating a grotto-like atmosphere. After being designated a degenerate artist by the Nazis for his abstract expressionist paintings, he left Germany in 1938. The original *Merzbau* was destroyed by Allied bombing during WWII, and we are only left with a few photographs. Schwitters eventually built two similar spaces in Norway and London.

Another early model for future installations was the 1938 International Surrealist Exhibition in Paris, which provided an opportunity for artists to redecorate the entire gallery to meet their unique aesthetic. Marcel Duchamp, Man Ray, Salvadore Dalí, and others transformed the grandiose gallery where their work would be displayed by obliterating the overhead sunlight with 1,200 dirty coal sacks hanging from the ceiling and scattering leaves and bits of cork over the floor. The smell of roasting coffee filled the air. Ray said that the recorded sounds of hysterical inmates in an insane asylum "cut short any desire on the part of visitors to laugh and joke." Dalí created a pond with water lilies surrounded by reeds, moss, rosebushes, and ferns. A rumpled Louis XV-style bed sat at each of the four corners of the gallery. The atmosphere was even more interesting opening night when the lighting failed, and visitors were forced to walk around with flashlights.

Marcel Duchamp contributed to an exhibition in New York City, called *First Papers of Surrealism* in 1942, by winding a mile-long string around the gallery amongst the paintings on the wall and across viewing space. The mess of string represented the challenge many people experience as they attempt to understand modern painting. To add to the chaos of the string maze, Duchamp asked a bunch of children to come to the opening and play active, noisy games, like ball and skip rope. Some guests complained of the noise, but Duchamp avoided the discord by not coming to the event.

With the 1960's came an atmosphere ripe for the development of installations as an defined art form. Inspired by the death of Jackson Pollock in 1956 and his studies with John Cage, Allan Kaprow (American, 1927-2006) began to develop concepts leading to his Happenings in 1961 and 1962 that required the viewer to be involved and not just an observer. He wrote:

> Not satisfied with the suggestion through paint of our senses, we shall utilize the specific substances of sight, sound, movement, people, odours, touch. Objects of every sort are materials for the new art: paint, chairs, food, electric and neon lights, smoke, water, old socks, a dog, movies, a thousand other things.

Kaprow rejected the conventional art gallery as the proper place for a new generation of artists, since that rather formal atmosphere encouraged the viewer to respond in the reverential old way. The gallery was also a market-oriented environment that Kaprow rejected, to be replaced by immersive spaces using second-hand materials and found objects that couldn't be sold.

James Turrell (American, b. 1943) began experimenting with light in the 1960s in immersive environments, which evolved into works such as *The Color Inside*, a room on the top of the Student Activity Center at the University of Texas, Austin. He describes his work as "where imaginative seeing and outside seeing meet, where it becomes difficult to differentiate between seeing from the inside and seeing from the outside."

Figure 12.1 Yellow phase, James Turrell, *The Color Inside*, 2013. University of Texas, Student Activity Center, Austin.

Figure 12.2 Pink phase, James Turrell, *The Color Inside*, 2013. University of Texas, Student Activity Center, Austin.

When sitting along the interior walls of the UT installation shortly before sunset or sunrise, one watches the hole in the ceiling as the sky shifts color with the changing projected light around it. Note how the sky in Figure 12.1 appears primary blue when yellow is projected around the opening and more of a gray when pink is projected. The dramatic change in the color of the sky is apparently caused partly by the persistence of vision that occurs when you look from one color to another. On the other hand, it just seems like magic. Turrell says that "perception is the object and the objective" of his art.

Bruce Nauman (American, b. 1941) is another of the seminal installation artists who used light. In *Green Light Corridor* 1970-1971, he forced the viewer to experience physical discomfort by creating a very narrow passageway that must be entered sideways. Oppressive green fluorescent lights

Meeting Twelve: Installation Art and Legacy

blasted at the visitor and left a magenta afterglow once out of the piece. Nauman wanted the visitor to be "activated" and disorientated, thus able to explore what it means to be human.

In many ways *Womanhouse* organized by Judy Chicago and Miriam Shapiro in 1972 seems closer to the Surrealism Exhibition, with an overlay of feminism, than it does to Nauman and Turrell's installations. Sited within an old mansion in Hollywood, *Womanhouse* represented twenty-eight women artists' take on the female's place within the home and society. Each piece was integrated into the various rooms of the house, such as Sandy Orgel's *Linen Closet,* a statement about keeping up with the washing and ironing. In the piece, a female mannequin is trapped in a closet with one leg stepping out, a shelf cutting her off at the neck and two more across her torso. Another closet, full of shoes, addressed women's desire to be fashionable. Other rooms focused on issues such as menstruation, lipstick, and the womb. A life-size doll bride descended a staircase.

Womanhouse was the first feminist art project to receive national attention. Some believed it "undermined aesthetic standards" and was more therapy than art. However, its influence on the development of installation art is clear.

Judy Chicago went on to create the iconic *Dinner Party*, which opened in 1979 at the San Francisco Museum of Modern Art. Comprised of thirteen place settings on each of the three 46.5-foot sides of a triangular table, the piece calls our attention to the lives of significant mythical and historical women.

While Chicago had a core staff, most of the 400 people who contributed to the project were volunteers, each paying $175, and arranging their own housing and meals. All were required to work forty hours per week and attend feminist education sessions.

Each table setting consists of a ceramic plate representing the historical period and life of each woman, a chalice, flatware, napkin, and a runner with the woman's name and related decorative borders, usually embroidered. However, the one for Hypatia (Alexandria, 370-415 AD) included Coptic tapestry weaving techniques and iconography. Elizabeth Eakins wove the bands of hearts on the edges, which referenced the bands on Coptic tunics. Jan Marie DuBois wove the two ends of the runner, but unfortunately the larger tapestry piece hangs inside the table in one of the corners where it is more difficult to see.

While some of the imagery of abortion and representation of vaginas in *The Dinner Party* has created controversy, fifteen million people around the world have been exposed to its exquisite craftsmanship and feminist message. It is now on permanent exhibition at the Brooklyn Museum, New York.

Installations of the 1980s began to include video, such as Bruce Nauman's *Learned Helplessness in Rats (Rock and Roll Drummer)* 1988, which included a video projection on the wall and a video monitor on each end of a Plexiglas maze on the floor. Images rotate between the three, but not in synch with each other, of a punk-rock drummer playing loudly, a frantic rat in the maze, and a live-feed on the maze showing the feet of the visitors as they pass by.

Clearly the theme is frustration. Nauman's thoughts on beauty in art, particularly in this piece, are instructive:

> I'm surprised when the work appears beautiful, and very pleased. And I think work can be very good and very successful without being able to call it beautiful, although I'm not clear about that. The work is good when it has a certain completeness, and when it's got a certain

Innovative Weaving

completeness, then it's beautiful. So I'm not sure how I'm seeing that. But maybe this has more of a traditional idea of beauty. It's a very pleasurable sensation.

Just as Nauman included the actions of the visitor within *Learned Helplessness*, much of the work by Ernesto Neto (Brazil, b. 1964) invites people to participate by touching and climbing inside. His installations, internationally recognized in the 1990's, are soft and biomorphic, usually crocheted forms stuffed with Styrofoam pellets and occasionally aromatic spices, hung from the ceiling. While Neto may represent a turning point, where installation art doesn't always come with an earnest message, but he still has much to say:

> My work speaks of the finite and the infinite, of the macroscopic and the microscopic, the internal and the external, by the masculine and feminine powers, but sex is like a snake, it slithers through everything.

HALO AMOK 2013 (an anagram of Oklahoma) by Wayne White (American, 1957) also incorporates the features we now expect in installation art. White created the piece specifically for the Oklahoma City Museum of Art as an interpretation of the Oklahoma cowboy. A rodeo bull rider, bronco rider, calf roper, and a cowboy on a high horse are constructed of cardboard, Styrofoam, wood, and simple machinery. Visitors are to pull on ropes and turn cranks to cause the sculptures to kick, trot, and make noise.

Installation Art Today

The popularity of installation art in the early 21st Century was demonstrated by the abundance of examples in Washington, DC, during 2015, such as the Smithsonian Institution's Arthur M. Sackler Gallery exhibition of *Filthy Lucre* by Darren Waterston (American, b. 1965). The piece is a reworking of James McNeill Whistler's Peacock Room on permanent display in the Freer Gallery next door. The original room was part of the London home owned by the wealthy shipping mogul Frederick Richards Leyland.

Figure 12.3 James McNeill Whistler, Peacock Room, 1876 and 1877. Freer Gallery of Art., Smithsonian Institution, Washington, DC

Figure 12.4 Darren Waterson, *Filthy Lucre*, 2014. Sackler Gallery, Smithsonian Institution, Washington, DC.

While Leland was out of town and without approval, Whistler painted the dining room completely in blue and gold patterns inspired by peacock feathers. Leyland returned home, angry at Whistler's initiative, refused to pay for the effort, and their friendship was forever ruptured.

Meeting Twelve: Installation Art and Legacy

When Darren Waterston (American, b. 1965) was asked to create a mural originally for the Massachusetts Museum of Contemporary Art in North Adams, MA, he thought of the Peacock Room and envisioned "a painting that one would literally 'walk into,' completely surrounding the viewer in the experience." The result is a room of damaged paintings on the wall, broken shelves, dripping paint, and shattered ceramics that represent the corruptive powers of money over art, with both the creators and the patrons being equally complicit.

An installation inspired by a book in most weaver's library, Marguerite Porter Davison's *A Handweaver's Pattern Book*, 1944, was included in the *Women in Art, Craft, and Design Midcentury and Today* exhibition at National Museum of Women in the Arts. Polly Apfelbaum (American, b. 1955) displayed her *Handweaver's Pattern Book,* comprised of 50 three-by-five-foot panels of silk velvet colored in dot patterns hung in two rows. Davison's patterns provided a jumping off point for Apfelbaum, who used a felt tip marker and a stencil to create the arranged dots.

Figure 12.5 Polly Apfelbaum. *Handweaver's Pattern Book* installation, 2014. National Museum of Women in the Arts, Washington, DC. Courtesy of the artist and Clifton Benevento.

Figure 12.6 Detail from *Handweaver's Pattern Book,* Polly Apfelbaum.

The original installation at the Clifton Benevento Gallery, New York City, in 2014, included ceramic beads hanging from the ceiling, with light creating shadows of a dot pattern on the floor. Visitors were required to weave amongst the threads as they moved around the room. Likely concerned about a possible safety hazard and holes in the ceiling, the Women's Museum chose to hang the beads in front of the panels and behind metal foot barriers, where they made less sense and appeared to be merely an attempt to create a third dimension. The placement of the beads also seems to change the piece from an installation expression to one of a more traditional display of textiles.

An art fair, rather than a museum, called Artomatic 2015, provided another opportunity to view installations. Artomatic takes advantage of empty buildings around the DC area and close to Metro stops to provide space for any artist who will pay a $125 fee and volunteer for three five-hour shifts. There are no judges, all artists are welcome. The 2015 event took place in an office building in Hyattsville, MD, with many different types of spaces, allowing interesting opportunities for installations, along with other visual art forms, including performance.

Leigh-Ann Friedel, who says she "creates installations, experiences, and everything in-between," collaborated with the sound engineer Jeffrey Dorfman to create *The Studio*. All four walls of an office space were painted in blue and white as if they were an architectural blueprint. A few objects stand out from the wall, such as a bird and a typewriter, calling for you to press them to hear Dorfman's soundscape.

Figure 12.7 Leigh-Ann Friedel and Jeffrey Dortman, *The Studio*. Artomatic 2015, Hyattsville, MD.

Innovative Weaving

Friedel represents the spirit behind installation art when she says in her artist statement "With a background in set design, she is passionate about site-specific work and ephemeral works."

Another installation at Artomatic was *Airing Dirty Laundry A Life Exposed* by Howard Thomas Hay, who has been collecting t-shirts since college in the early 1970s. In his artist statement he says that the 1955 washing machine in the work represents the womb, with the time line of his life played out in the shirts hung with wooden clothespins. The clothesbasket at the far end of the display represents "the end of my life, like a casket." Populist events such as Artomatic provide an opportunity for people like Hay, whose idea has been boiling for over forty years, to express their creativity without going through the usual gauntlet of exhibition jurors.

Figure 12.8 Howard Thomas May, *Airing Dirty Laundry*, 2015. Artomatic, Hyattsville, MD.

In contrast, the Smithsonian Institution's Renwick Gallery, which specializes in craft and decorative arts, presented installations from nine well-known and respected contemporary artists for its November 2015 reopening. *Plexus A1* by Gabriel Dawe (Mexico, b. 1973) is one of a long series of similar constructions with embroidery thread and hooks. His choice to use thread as a medium was an attempt to "explore and subvert social constructs of gender." As a child, he wanted to embroider like his sister, but was intimidated by the machismo of the Mexican culture.

Figure 12.9 Gabriel Dawe. *Plexus A1* (detail), 2015, thread, wood, hoods and steel. Part of the 2015 exhibition *WONDER* at the Renwick Gallery of the Smithsonian American Art Museum, Washington DC. *Wonder*, 2015.

Eventually, I came to see the structures I was making with thread as symbolic representation of these social constructs, the viewer navigating and negotiating the installation in a dance that is analogous to what we do in real life, without any particular thought.

Figure 12.10 Jennifer Angus. *In the Midnight Garden* (detail), 2015, cochineal, various insects, and mixed media. Part of the 2015 exhibition *WONDER* at the Renwick Gallery of the Smithsonian American Art Museum, Washington, DC.

An installation can fill a room almost to the walls or be the walls, as in the work of Jennifer Angus (Canada, b. 1961), who has been decorating rooms with large insects since 2003. Say what? Yes, with non-endangered bugs from Malaysia, Thailand, and Papua New Guinea placed in patterns reminiscent of Victorian wallpaper. In the Renwick, she stained the walls with cochineal dye to create a lovely pink wash effect. The cabinet of drawers in the middle of the room was reminiscent of 19th century insect collections. A wasp nest bobbed from a branch at the top of the cabinet

She says: "Something I am trying to capture in my work is the magic we experience as children. I would like people to discover it once again when they see my work, and for a moment just stand there and say "Wow!."

Meeting Twelve: Installation Art and Legacy

Nature out of place can also be found in John Grade's *Middle Fork (Cascades)*, 2015. Grade created a plaster cast from a standing 150-year-old hemlock tree he found in the Cascade Mountains of Washington State. Comprised of a half-million segments of reclaimed cedar, the enormous trunk and its sectioned branches are suspended from the ceiling, floating independently above the floor, yet appearing tragic lying on its side in a room barely large enough to hold it. Hundreds of volunteers and paid staff built the piece in Seattle over a year's time.

Figure 12.11 John Grade. *Middle Fork (Cascades)*, (detail), 2015, reclaimed old-growth western red cedar. Part of the 2015 exhibition *WONDER* at the Renwick Gallery of the Smithsonian American Art Museum, Washington, DC.

Maya Lin also addressed nature in her *Folding the Chesapeake*, 2015, but with glass marbles glued down to represent the Chesapeake Bay watershed. The work flows across the floor and up three walls of the gallery space. Lin says that "The piece allows me to give people an idea of the totality. You see [the Chesapeake Bay] as a single organism, as a living organism."

Figure 12.12 Maya Lin. *Folding the Chesapeake* (detail), 2015, marbles and adhesive. Part of the 2015 exhibition *WONDER* at the Renwick Gallery of the Smithsonian American Art Museum, Washington, DC.

While Lin expressed the fragility of Nature, Janet Echelman was inspired by its tremendous power. Her knotted and braided sculpture *1.8*, 2015, hanging above printed textile flooring on the second level of the Renwick, represented the devastating Tohoku earthquake, tsunami, and resulting Fukushima nuclear power disaster in March 2011.

The piece used 50 miles of string and about 500,000 knots. Lighting, programmed to slowly shift colors, forces the viewer to linger, rather than merely move into the next gallery. A year after the Chilean earthquake represented by Echerman's *1.26* shown in Figure 10.8, her Renwick installation, *1.8*, references the effect of the earth being shifted on its axis by the Japanese quake, causing March 11, 2011, to be shortened by yet another 1.8 millionths of a second.

An installation piece was one of the highlights of WSSA's participation in the WEST Austin Studio Tour in 2016. Since 2012, a member's home has been the temporary studio/clubhouse for the guild during the tour. For the exercise of the last meeting of the Innovative Weaving study group, the members brainstormed the idea of an installation for the event that followed five months later. The piece, entitled *The Loom Room*, would take over one of the bedrooms. Some of the generated ideas that ended up in the installation, with minor adjustments, were:

- A large loom dominating the room

Innovative Weaving

- Felted dyepot with flames underneath
- Paper covering bookshelves in the room with clever fiber-related take offs of book titles, such as "*Little Weaving Women* by Louisa May Lostmycount."
- Weaving-related quotations in cartoon bubbles on the wall
- A backstrap loom and partial weaving
- A clock showing how much time a weaver spends on different tasks
- A flyer outside the room reporting a missing cat, with a picture of a toy cat
- The toy cat wrapped up in the cloth beam
- A life-size doll with chocolate on his face and hands touching the warp
- Warp wrapped all around the room, including up over a trapeze and the ceiling fan, to show chaos, but also to restrict movement further into the room
- A recorded loop of the sounds of an active studio that included the repeating sound of a beater and interruptions, like the doorbell and someone asking when dinner would be ready.
- Bulletin board full of meetings, ideas, etc.
- Chiropractor appointment slip stuck to the loom.
- Broken coffee cup with spilled coffee covering weaving draft on the floor

Figure 12.13 *The Loom Room*, WSSA Innovative Weaving Study Group, 2016. WEST Austin Studio Tour, Austin, Texas.

The piece proved to be the perfect final project for the study group, reinforcing the significance and possibilities of installation art, while also allowing nine of its members to collaborate. The creative process was illustrated as the effort evolved from Open Creativity ideas to Focused Creativity practicality. Giggles and praises of the visitors demonstrated the *Loom Room*'s success.

From the experienced to the first-timers, all of these installation artists have shown the power of filling entire rooms with large social, environmental, and political ideas, as well as with more personal issues.

Consider Your Legacy

Like an artist of any medium, most people creating installations want to share their vision and/or experience with others. And the artists want their work and ideas to be remembered and not forgotten as soon as the viewer leaves the room. As weavers, our work always makes an impact, whether on the earth's resources, on the emotions of friends and family, on the artistic sensibilities of people we don't know, and our own sense of accomplishment and satisfaction. The following section suggests ways to help our work have positive impacts and continue to be appreciated for many generations to come.

Meeting Twelve: Installation Art and Legacy

Documentation

Art historians, art lovers, and artists alike all relish delving into the artistic process. What was the initial inspiration? What changed from the first inspiration to the final? How does the piece fit into the artist's full body of work? The Sackler Gallery answered those questions and more for *Filthy Lucre* with its display of Darren Waterston's studies as part of the exhibit. While Waterston's theme of art and its corruption by money helps us understand his inspiration for the installation piece, his studies demonstrate an accomplished painter highly skilled in his craft and one determined to bring his artistic vision to every detail of the work.

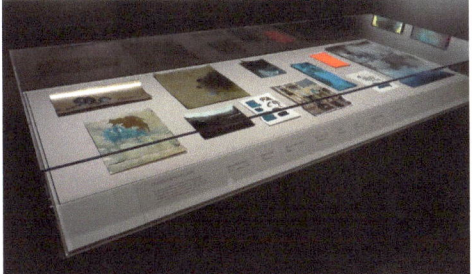

Figure 12.14 Darren Waterston. Studies for *Filthy Lucre*, 2014. Smithsonian Institution Sackler Gallery.

Your own work also deserves to be documented. Saving your own inspiration notebooks, studies, drawdowns, and samples may help future weavers expand their own work. Thus consider handing down your notebooks to your guild's library. Attaching a note to a special piece can help bring it to life once you are unable to tell its story. Figure 12.15 shows a tablecloth over 200 years old made by Letitia Huey (American, 1798-1879) and a note that says:

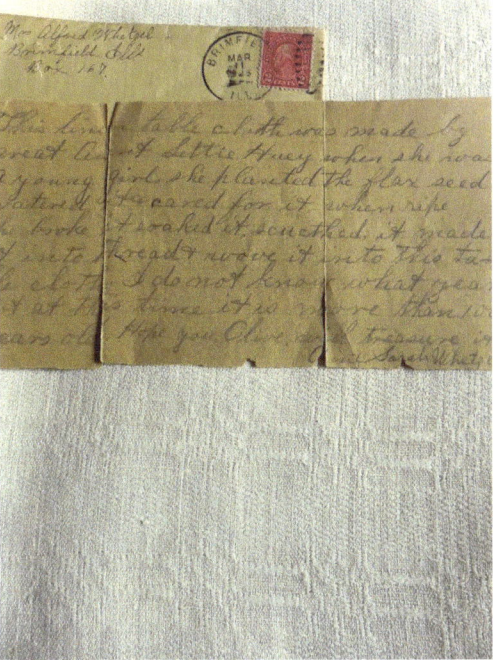

Figure 12.15 Letitia Huey, Linen Tablecloth, c. 1810, and documentation, 1925..

> This linen table cloth was made by great Aunt Lettie Huey when she was a young girl. She planted the flax seed, watered and cared for it, when ripe she broke it, soaked it, scucthed [sic] and made it into thread and wove it into this tablecloth. I do not know what year but at this time it is more than 100 years old. Hope you, Olive, will treasure it.
>
> Aunt Sarah Whetzel
> Brimfield, Illinois
> 1925

The more information you provide about your work, the better chance it will continue to be cherished for many years. Weave, embroider, or pen in your name and year on the more important pieces. Title, town, materials, and inspiration on an attached acid-free card will help bring your work to life for future generations.

Lasting Emotional Response/Memories

Our emotional reaction to a work of art affects how well we remember it. Will viewers continue to think and talk about your work or merely pass it by with indifference? The value of the artist statement to make a connection is illustrated by the labeling of Gabriel Dawe's installation piece at the Renwick (Figure 12.9). His website describes his frustration with gender roles, specifically the machismo atmosphere in his home country of Mexico that discouraged his interest in embroidery. It is easy to imagine that many visitors would be more affected by an artist statement that

Innovative Weaving

described his work as a symbolic representation of our dance around gender roles, rather than the more neutral one in *Wonder* that said the piece was inspired by memories of the skies in Mexico and East Texas and the colors of Mexican embroideries.

Making people smile or laugh can also help ensure your work is memorable. Wayne White is well known for his work as puppeteer and set designer for *Pee-Wee's Playhouse* in the mid-1980s. Around 2000, he began to paint stylized words over landscape reproductions he found in thrift stores. One seascape has four signs receding toward the horizon, with the following messages: "Just a Picture," "shunned by scholars," "now it costs," "10,000 dollars." When asked about these works, White said:

> I'd like it to be thought of on different levels. Definitely there's art history in there, it's not just a goof. I take it very seriously and I take the skill very seriously, but ultimately I do want it to be funny. I do want the humor. The best comedy is multi-leveled.
>
> The great stand-ups were all very deep: Richard Pryor, George Carlin -- all of those guys. Their humor is hilarious but also moving, intelligent. It hits a lot of notes beyond just the laugh. But the laugh is such an irresistible thing for me: It lets you know that you've communicated.
>
> People discount humor. They think tragedy and suffering and being bummed out is what real intelligence is. But no, man. It's way harder to get a laugh than to bum somebody out.

Figure 12.16 Mary Macaulay, *Lucky Fish Hat*, 2014. Wool felt.

Mary Macaulay, a WSSA member, creates felt hats that are well-made and fun to wear, yet have thoughtful artistic content. While potential customers may giggle as they try on a orange hat with red spikes poking out the top or a white one with three felted rocks at the crown, each of her hats comes from "deep within my soul." For example, one hat with a single large fish hooked to the crown developed as Macaulay was processing the recent death of her mother, who loved to fish.

She finds that an idea might seem fun as she works on it, but she is definitely not trying to be "funny," she wants her work to be seen as creative, not just humorous. Like Wayne White, Macaulay takes her themes and craftsmanship very seriously. That depth and multitude of layers help ensure that the viewer walks away somehow touched by her work.

Effects on the Environment

Insensitive use of nonrenewable resources is one thing in a small art piece, but such thoughtlessness becomes more significant in a large installation. Without considering the impact of one's art on the environment, an artist might find viewers distracted by negative reactions to the work and thus miss the intended message. For instance, a hundred years ago Jennifer Angus would not have felt a need to justify her profuse use of insects in her work. However, in 2015, she included a sentence in her artist statement assuring the visitor that the insects were not endangered.

Meeting Twelve: Installation Art and Legacy

Degradable materials are a major theme in the work of John Grade. The ephemeral nature of the cedar sculpture at the Renwick is essential to his message and his art. When the *Wonder* show is over, all the small cedar pieces of *Middle Fork (Cascades)* will be taken apart and placed at the base of the old hemlock tree used as the model. Grade will document the process with photos and videos, which will be the longest-lasting legacy of his work, rather than in the work itself. Of course, the memories of the people who helped build the work and those who saw it in person are also part of its legacy.

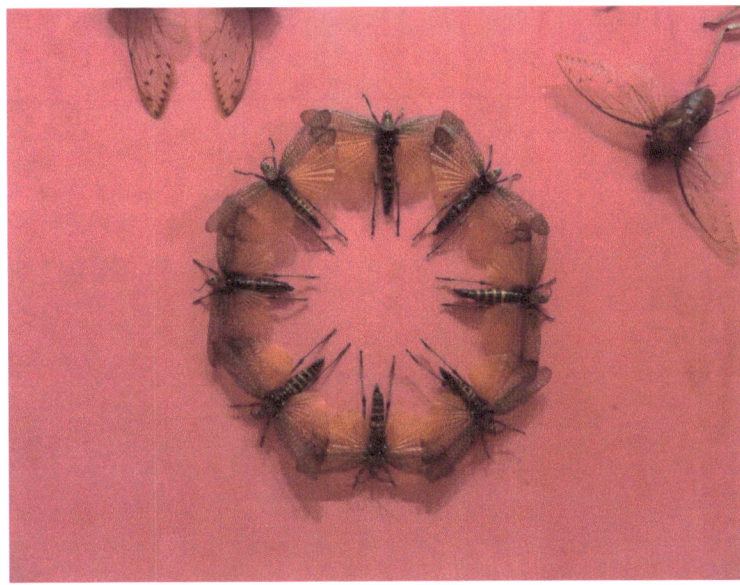

Figure 12.17 Jennifer Angus. *In the Midnight Garden* (detail), 2015, cochineal, various insects, and mixed media. Part of the 2015 exhibition WONDER at the Renwick Gallery of the Smithsonian American Art Museum, Washington, DC.

Your choice of materials and equipment help define who you are as an artist and are not to be made without thought. Some people may be drawn to your work because of the materials you use, such as Pam James' recycled yarns, and others may reject your gorgeous shawl simply because it contains fiber made from nonrenewable resources. These rather abstract qualities of your work may seem trivial, but are, in fact, part of your legacy.

Social Media

Artists no longer need to depend upon a publisher to distribute photos of their work in a book or magazine. And gone are the days when all artists felt a need to prevent the public (and fellow artists) from photographing their work. Weavolution, Twitter, Snapchat, Instagram, Facebook, and your own website provide opportunities to share your work. *The Studio* artist, Leigh-Ann Friedel, welcomed viewers to photograph her work at Artomatic, but asked that they attach hash tags (#the studio and #artomatic2015) when sharing on Twitter. She recognized the advantages of encouraging visitors to advertise her work. You will likely find that embracing web access to your work is more satisfying and productive then worrying about people stealing your ideas.

Souvenirs

Sometimes opportunities arise that allow you to share a tangible reminder of your work with visitors. For instance, Duchamp bought sixteen miles of string, but used only one in *One Mile of String*. During installation one mile caught fire. He gave the rest away and said "It made someone very happy—a kind of insurance, string enough to last him the rest of his life."

When 168,000 glass marbles were purchased for Maya Lin's piece at the Renwick and only 54,000 were used, the Gallery gave out small sacks of the leftovers to children the weekend after the opening. Many of those kids will treasure that gift into their adulthood as a reminder of Lin's installation.

Innovative Weaving

Exercises

The first exercise helps you start the process of developing an installation piece somewhere in your community. The second one encourages you to think about your own legacy.

Exercise 12.1 (30 minutes)

Ten Minutes What space would be appropriate for an installation piece? How might you alone or in collaboration with others use weaving as the core medium to fill the specified space?

Twenty Minutes One at a time, share your ideas for a space and how you would you fill it.

Exercise 12.2 (30 minutes)

Ten Minutes Write down who you see as the most important person(s) to receive your creative legacy and what do you want to pass on to them.

Twenty Minutes One at a time, share two or three of your ideas with the group and note any subsequent ideas that come to mind.

Conclusion

Installation art provides not only an opportunity to surround the viewer with big ideas, but it also presents ways to involve the viewer more directly in your work. However, the more immersive your idea, the more likely you come up with aspects of the installation that are outside your skill set or are too time consuming. Rather than cutting back on your concept, consider collaborating with other artists, skilled workers, friends, and neighbors. Let your vision blossom.

Whether you take on an installation project or not, consider the legacy of all your work. Take photos, sign your work, and document the inspiration and design process. Share your work at guild show-and-tells, on social media, and at shows, conferences, and galleries. Include artist statements when appropriate to let people know what inspired you. Your creativity touches every one who sees your work and, most important, is a reminder to yourself to keep weaving to keep the joy flowing.

Further Sources for Inspiration

Elizabeth Gilbert, *Big Magic; Creative living beyond fear*. New York: Riverhead Books, 2015.

Debbie Herd, "Coptic Tapestry and Looking to the Past." Search web.

Claire Bishop, *Installation Art*. London: Tate Publishing, 2005.

AFTERWORD

This study guide should be only a beginning of your exploration into the art forms and artists that we have covered here. Take advantage of every opportunity to visit a new art exhibit (or old one) and watch documentaries about artists of all mediums, paying attention to what inspires them and how they incorporate that inspiration into their work. Read, read, read about musicians, painters, actors, filmmakers, sculptors, dancers, writers, and creators of all types. You will learn more about your own kind. No, your name or work may not be as well known, but we all share that drive to create.

In the final weeks of writing this study guide, Elizabeth Gilbert's book *Big Magic; Creative Living Beyond Fear* was released. She has so much to say about what we all struggle with as weavers, such as "You can measure your worth by your dedication to your path, not by your successes or failures" and "Creativity is a gift to the creator, not just a gift to the audience." And possibly of most importance to remember, "The guardians of high culture will try to convince you that the arts belong only to a chosen few, but they are wrong and they are annoying. We are *all* the chosen few."

So go out there and create outside the box, relish the weird and wonderful idea that just came to mind and risk going where your ideas take you. With shuttle in hand and a warp ahead, you have all that is needed for a joyous and creative life as a weaver.

Innovative Weaving

ACKNOWLEDGEMENTS

First I have to give my appreciation to the board of the Weavers and Spinners Society of Austin for their faith that we could get through this project together. The members of the study group stuck it out through the twelve months of meetings, reading each chapter as it came hot off the press, sometimes less than a week before the meeting, acting as guinea pigs for the brainstorming exercises, sharing projects they made inspired by the chapters, and arguing, with no conclusion, the definitions of artist and craftsperson.

This would be a visually boring book without the generosity of all the innovative artists that shared their images.

A big thanks to the readers: Inga Marie Carmel, Alice K. McWilliams, Larry Stuebing, and DeeDee Woodbury. Also thanks to the subject matter experts: Tom Gingras, Ann S. Graham, Jeff Ryder, Nikos Salingaros, and again Larry Stuebing. Madelyn van der Hoogt read a couple of chapters early on and gave me the encouragement to keep going and to self-publish. My conversations with Kelly Guerrero and Lynn Putney were invaluable as they helped me sort through what it means to be an artist.

Sincere appreciation must go to my first weaving teacher, Carolyn Atwater, and my first spinning teacher, Sylvia DeMar, at Springwater Fiber Workshop, in Alexandria, Virginia, not only for the technical skills they taught me, but also for introducing me to the wonderful, supportive large community of weavers and spinners.

Innovative Weaving

INDEX

3rd dimension, 30
Abromović, Marina, 71
Adams, Ansel, 90
AKIRASH, 71
Albers, Anni, 50
Angus, Jennifer, 142, 146
aperture, 91
Apfelbaum, Polly, 141
Arcangel, Cory, 131
architecture, 55
Art Snob, 77, 78
art vs craft, 64
artist, 64
artist statement, 82
asymmetry, 57
avant-garde film, 128
balance, 35, 58
Bass, Saul, 128
Bateman, Bob, 38, 59
bespoke, 105
Bono, 103
Bontecou, Lee, 37
borrowing, 48, 108
   Tidball guidelines, 49
brainstorming, 13, 26
   group flow, 73
   rules, 26
Burning Man, 72
Cage, John, 69
Carmel, Inga Marie, 96, 132
Catlin, George, 77
Cheatham, Andi Scull, 116
Chicago, Judy, 139
Choi+Shine, 116
Christo, 115
client relationship, 64
coherence, 61
collaboration
   conflict, 74
   location, 74
collection, 106
Collingwood, Peter, 36
color, 23
composition, 93, 127
concept, 79
consensus, 9
content, 24, 36, 77
contrast, 34
Cook, Lia, 83

copyright, 49
costume, 106
CowParade, 118
craftperson, 64
craftsmanship, 94
creativity
   definition, 15
   Focused, 18
   Open, 18
   preference quiz, 17
credits, opening, 128
crowdfunding, 122
Curtis, Nathaniel, 63
Curtis, Sandy, 29
Daguerre, Louis, 89
Davis, Arthur Q., 63
Dawe, Gabriel, 142, 145
detail, 33
dimension, 21
Dinner Party, 139
Doak, Sandra, 22
documentation, 145
Dorfman, Jeffrey, 142
Duchamp, Marcel, 138
dynamics, 44
Echelman, Janet, 119, 143
Edun, 103
environment, 146
environmental art, 115
Essig, Vicki, 83
facilitator, 10
Farley, Pam, 82
fashion, 101
feature film, 127
fiber art categories, 81
Fibonacci, Leonardo, 60
Fischinger, Oskar, 127
focus, 91
Friedel, Leigh-Ann, 141, 147
Fujimori, Terunobu, 64
function, 62
games, 130
Gargallo, Pablo, 35
Gaudi, Antoni, 57, 66
Gehry, Frank, 58, 61
genre, 47
Gilliam, Terry, 127
Gingras, Tom, 32
Goff, Bruce, 61, 66

Innovative Weaving

Goldsworthy, Andy, 115
Grade, John, 119, 143, 147
graffiti, 116
Grateful Dead, 69
Group f/64, 90
group flow, 73
guild project, 120, 143
Guitartown, 118
Halprin, Anna, 70
Halprin, Lawrence, 59
handmade, 105
Hanson, Erika Lynn, 83
harmony, 45
haute-couture, 103
Hay, Howard Thomas, 142
Hewson, Ali, 103
Hicks, Sheila, 31, 84
improvisation, 46
Inspiration Notebook, 14, 110
installation art, 137
Isermann, Jim, 33
ISO, 92
James, Pam, 110, 147
Jeanne-Claude, 115
Johnston, Robin, 78
Kaestner, Tracy, 43
Kaprow, Allan, 138
Kelman, Mo, 36
Kirchoff, Sharine, 96
Knisely, Tom, 135
Koehn, Molly, 15
Krizia, 32
Krone, Judith Powell, 45
Kurosawa, Akira, 127
La Lotería, 114
Lamb, Sara, 135
Lancaster, Daryl, 109, 135
land art, 115
Lanina, Yuliya, 121
Laskey, Ruth, 84
Le Corbusier, 60
legacy, 144
Lemmen, Georges, 24
Liebovitz, Annie, 94
light, 34
light shows, 131
Lin, Maya, 143, 147
line, 23
Macaulay, Mary, 80, 146
made to measure, 105
Marshall, John, 93
Marshall, Rilla, 84
mass, 32
mass market, 104
McCardell, Clair, 102

McQueen, Alexander, 103
melody, 43
Mies van der Rohe, Ludwig, 63
Miyake, Issey, 102
Monger, Sarah, 93
Montemayor, Wanda, 114
Moon, Beth, 94
Morgan, Julia, 65
motion, 132
moving pictures, 125
Muñoz, Aurèlia, 16
murals, 114
music, 41
National Endowment for the Arts, 121
Nauman, Bruce, 138
Oak Forest Stitch and Bitch, 118
Olek, Crocheted, 117
Ono, Yoko, 70
Orr, Lisa, 114
Otterness, Tom, 119
Paik, Nam June, 129
painting, 21
passion, 77, 79
pattern, 59
Peacock Room, 140
Pei, I.M., 60
performance, 69
perseverance, 122
Persig, Robert, 15
Peters, Bernadette, 45
photography, 89
Pollack, Jackson, 77
Prêt-à-porter, 104
proportion, 33, 60, 67
   Salingaros rules, 62
public art, 113
public art programs, 121
Putney, Lynn, 22, 23
ready-to-wear, 104
resolution, 46
rhythm, 44, 59
   at the loom, 50
Ricketts, Rowland, 84
Riis, Jon Eric, 30
risk, 36
runway, 108
Salingaros, Nikos, 60, 62, 67
Sanders, Jeremy Chase, 85
Saori, 25, 105
Savile Row, 105
Sayeg, Magda, 117
scale, 60
Schira, Cynthia, 86
Schneider, Bob, 47
Schwitters, Kurt, 137

sculpture, 29, 118
Semper, Gottfried, 55
series, 106, 109, 110
shadow, 34
shape, 22
Shapiro, Miriam, 139
Shapton, Leanne, 128
shutter speed, 92
Sondheim, Stephen, 42, 46
space, 32
study group
    organizing, 9
style, 25
support, 35
symmetry, 57
synaesthesia, 85
tailoring, 105
television, 129
tempo, 43
tension, 46
texture, 22
    contrast, 33
The Gates, 116
theme, 61
Tider, Andrew, 120
timbre, 45
tone, 42
Turrell, James, 138

Umlauf, Charles, 30
unity, 62
value, 24
van Herpen, Iris, 132
Vandermeiden, Jette, 50, 135
variation, 61
variety, 62
video, 129, 131
viewing angle, 30
Vitruvius, 56
volume, 44
Walther, Franz Erhard, 70
Waterston, Darren, 140, 145
wearable art, 106
Weavers and Spinners Society of Austin, 7, 143
    CHT performance, 75
Wechsler, Steve, 132
Whistler, James McNeill, 140
white balance, 92
White, Wayne, 140, 146
Wiley, Kehinde, 129
Winter, Katie, 97
Womanhouse, 139
WSSA. *See* Weavers and Spinners Society of Austin
yarnbombing, 117
Yeatts, Linda, 34, 58, 80